Social Patterns in Normal Aging

Social Patterns in Normal Aging: Findings from the Duke Longitudinal Study

Erdman Palmore

Duke University Press   Durham, North Carolina   1981

Library of Congress Cataloging in Publication Data

Palmore, Erdman Ballagh, 1930-
  Social patterns in normal aging.

  Bibliography: p.
  Includes index.
  1. Aging—Social aspects—United States—
Longitudinal studies. I. Title.
HQ1064.U5P26   305.2'6   81-9800
ISBN 0-8223-0458-9   AACR2

To our children and grandchildren,
who help make our aging so satisfying.

Contents

List of Tables and Figures   ix

Foreword   xi

Chapter 1. Introduction   3

Purpose   3

Major Issues   3

The Duke Longitudinal Studies   7

Methods of Analysis   11

Summary   13

Chapter 2. Socioeconomic Status   15

Aging Effects   15

Factors Affecting Socioeconomic Status   22

Effects of Socioeconomic Status   24

Summary   31

Chapter 3. Retirement   32

Age, Period, and Cohort Effects   32

Determinants of Retirement   34

Consequences of Retirement   39

Summary   45

Chapter 4. Social Activity   47

Aging Effects   47

Factors Affecting Social Activity   54

Consequences of Social Activity   59

Summary   65

Chapter 5. Social Networks   67

Age, Period, and Cohort Effects   67

Antecedents   73

Consequences   79

Summary   80

Chapter 6. Sexual Behavior   83
Aging Effects   83
Antecedents   89
Consequences   92
Summary   106

Chapter 7. Life Satisfaction   95
Aging Effects   95
Antecedents   99
Consequences   104
Summary   106

Chapter 8. Conclusion   108
Major Issues   108
Implications   114

Appendix. Variables in the Longitudinal Studies   117

Bibliography   127
Index   132

Figures and Tables

Figures

3-1. *Percentage not employed by year and sex*   35
3-2. *Percentage retired by age cohort and sex (rounds 1 to 4)*   36
4-1. *Total intimate contacts and leisure activities scores for pairs of rounds by year and sex*   50
4-2. *Number of social hours by age cohort and sex II (rounds 1 to 4)*   51
4-3. *Number of church and club meetings attended by age and sex*   54
5-1. *Percentage married and living with spouse by sex and year*   71
5-2. *Percentage married by age cohort and sex (rounds 1 to 4)*   72
6-1. *Percentage of married men and women sexually active (rounds 1 to 5)*   85
6-2. *Frequency of intercourse among sexually active married men and women (rounds 1 to 5)*   86
6-3. *Percentage of married men and women sexually active, by mean age for four cohorts (rounds 1 to 4)*   87
6-4. *Frequency of sex relations among sexually active married men and women by age cohort (rounds 1 to 4)*   88
7-1. *Life satisfaction and happiness for pairs of rounds by sex*   97
7-2. *Change in life satisfaction by age and sex cohorts (rounds 1 to 4)*   98
7-3. *Change in anomie by age and sex cohorts (rounds 1 to 4)*   99

Tables

1-1. *Participants in the first longitudinal study by round*   8
1-2. *Participants in the second longitudinal study by round*   10
1-3. *Characteristics of participants compared with nonparticipants*   10
1-4. *Characteristics of study sample compared with U.S. white persons aged 45-69*   11
2-1. *Occupational distribution by age as reported in the second longitudinal study*   18
2-2. *Occupational distribution by age as reported in the first longitudinal study*   18
2-3. *Mean income by age, period, and cohort*   19
2-4. *Present financial position compared to age 55 by age group*   20
2-5. *Mean economic security by age, period, and cohort*   20
2-6. *Subjective class identification by age group*   21
2-7. *Mean score on the variable* respected *by age, period, and cohort*   21
2-8. *Feelings of status by age, period and cohort*   22
2-9. *Reduced form and complete equation for income of men aged 60-70: Standardized coefficients (beta)*   24
2-10. *Relation of socioeconomic status to health, intelligence, social activity, and satisfaction (second study)*   27
2-11. *Relation of socioeconomic status to health, intelligence, social activity, satisfaction (first study)*   28
2-12. *Significant effects of socioeconomic status on age changes*   30
3-1. *Percentage not in labor force by sex, age, period, and cohort (U.S.A.)*   33

3-2. *Reasons for retirement*   38

3-3. *Significant changes after retirement*   43

3-4. *Change in life satisfaction and affect balance after retirement*   44

3-5. *Multiple regression of significant predictors of life satisfaction after retirement*   45

4-1. *Comparison of present club and church attendance to age 55 attendance*   53

4-2. *Significant round 1 predictors of round 2 social activity, by sex (simple correlations)*   56

4-3. *Significant predictors of change in social activity from round 1 to round 2, by sex*   57

4-4. *Significant round 1 predictors of round 2 social activity, by sex (correlation matrix)*   58

4-5. *Significant predictors of change in social activity from round 1 to round 2, by sex*   59

4-6. *Significant round 1 activity predictors of round 2 consequences, by sex*   62

4-7. *Significant activity predictors of change in consequences, by sex*   62

4-8. *Significant round 1 activity predictors of round 2 consequences, by sex (correlation matrix)*   63

4-9. *Significant round 1 activity predictors of change in consequences*   63

4-10. *Significant predictors of longevity difference, by sex*   64

5-1. *Percentage married and living with spouse by sex, age, and year*   68

5-2. *Percentage living alone by sex, age, and year*   68

5-3. *Percentage of persons in social network who were in a younger catgory than the panelist, by sex and round*   73

5-4. *Significant predictors of social network variables, by sex (correlation matrix)*   75

5-5. *Significant predictors of change in social networks (residual change analysis)*   76

5-6. *Significant round 1 predictors of round 2 social network variables by sex (correlation matrix)*   77

6-1. *Patterns of sexual activity from round 1 to rounds 2 and 3 among married men and women*   89

6-2. *Patterns of sexual activity from round 1 to 4 among married men and women by age cohort*   90

6-3. *Round 1 predictors of round 4 frequency of sex relations (zero-order correlations)*   91

6-4. *Round 1 predictors of round 4 frequency of sex relations (step-wise multiple regression analysis)*   92

6-5. *Consequences of sexual activity for married men and women (correlation matrix)*   94

7-1. *Significant predictors of total life satisfaction and happiness attitudes for men and women (correlation matrix)*   101

7-2. *Multiple regression of significant predictors of life satisfaction*   102

7-3. *Significant predictors of life satisfaction, affect balance, and anomie (correlation matrix)*   103

7-4. *Significant predictors of life satisfaction (multiple regression)*   104

7-5. *Significant predictors of affect balance (multiple regression)*   104

7-6. *Significant predictors of anomie (multiple regression)*   105

7-7. *Significant consequences of life satisfaction indicators (correlation matrix)*   105

Foreword

Monday night, August 25, 1980, marked the end of an era at the Duke Center for the Study of Aging and Human Development. On this date a large number of research investigators who had been involved in the Duke Longitudinal Studies of Normal Aging, some for over two decades, met officially for the last time. The Monday Night Meetings of the longitudinal investigators had become a tradition under the leadership of E. W. Busse, M.D., the principal investigator of the pioneering, multidisciplinary, longitudinal studies of aging that had begun early in the 1950s.

The Longitudinal Studies are an important part of the Duke Center's history. These studies that covered over two decades documented some important scientific contributions to our understanding of aging, about how to study aging, and about how to share what is known about aging with scientific colleagues and the public. Substantively, the Duke Longitudinal Studies documented effectively a realistically optimistic view of adult life in all its variety. Older adults demonstrably have far greater biological, psychological, and social potential than had been imagined previously. Methodologically, the Duke Studies were in the forefront of demonstrating the scientific value of multidisciplinary, longitudinal research that highlighted the complex interaction of biomedical, behavioral, and social factors in aging. Duke investigators were also in the forefront in demonstrating how new data analysis techniques could help disentangle the relative importance of age, external events, and the particular experience of different groups of older adults; and our capacity to explain observed difference in the experience of aging was enhanced. The final report to the National Institute of Aging was submitted in 1980 with a sense of satisfaction in over a thousand scientific articles and other publications that shared with colleagues and the general public the basis of a new understanding of later life. The complete data sets of the Duke Longitudinal Studies, adequately documented, are now in the public domain and are available to the next generation of scholars through the Duke Center's Data Archive.

An era ends. An era begins. With the publication of this monograph on *Social Patterns in Normal Aging*, Professor Palmore presents the first of several monographs that will review systematically the findings of the Duke Longitudinal Studies from a variety of perspectives—biomedical, behavioral, social scientific, and methodological. This volume builds upon and integrates the work of dozens of colleagues in a variety of disciplines who shared with Professor Palmore a dedication not only to continuing the project and maintaining the data in useable form over many years but also to sharing their complementary disciplinary perspectives. Professor Palmore's sociological perspective on normal aging is immeasurably enriched by his association with colleagues in medicine, psychiatry, psychology, biostatistics, and computer sciences.

This book makes important contributions in its own right. Professor Palmore has been particularly effective in applying contemporary multivariate statistical techniques to complex issues of longitudinal data analysis. He has advanced our understanding of ways to disentangle the age/period/cohort effects, a problem that constitutes a central issue in contemporary gerontological research. He has advanced our understanding of the experience of aging among non-institutionalized older adults with normative data on patterns of activity, life satisfaction, and sexual behavior. His optimistic conclusions about the adaptive capacity of older adults in dealing with life events such as retirement, widowhood, and illness are well documented and reassuring.

The readable style of this volume will introduce the Duke Longitudinal Studies to the general public as well as to the scientific community. The stage has been set for additional systematic reports on the Duke Longitudinal studies of normal aging.

George L. Maddox, Ph.D.
    Center Director

March, 1981

Social Patterns in Normal Aging

Chapter 1. Introduction

Purpose

This book has two basic purposes: to review previous theories and findings on social patterns in normal aging, and to present findings from the Duke Longitudinal Studies of Aging relevant to these theories. The focus is on *normal* or typical aging rather than on unusual or pathological aging.

Gerontology is a relatively young science. Until the 1950s there were almost no professional gerontologists, no courses in gerontology, no centers on aging, and only one gerontological journal (*The Journal of Gerontology* began in 1946). Now there are over 5,000 professional members of the Gerontological Society, several thousand courses in gerontology, hundreds of centers on aging, six major journals in gerontology, and dozens of newsletters on aging. Because of this rapid growth, a large literature on social factors in aging has recently developed, and there is a need for systematic review of the theories and facts presented in this literature because such reviews at present are rare and rapidly become out of date. Thus we will begin each section of this book with a brief survey of the existing theories and the findings of previous studies.

Greater than the need for such review, however, is the need to systematically present the results of the Duke Longitudinal Studies relevant to the existing theories. The 1955-69 findings of the Duke Longitudinal Studies have been published in *Normal Aging* (Palmore, 1970), the 1970-73 findings in *Normal Aging II* (Palmore, 1974), and findings since 1973 have been presented in about forty articles and papers. This book is a systematic presentation and summary of all our major findings on social patterns in aging, and a discussion of their implications for major issues in the field.

Major Issues

The major issues in social gerontology relevant to the evidence from the Duke Longitudinal Studies can be grouped into five descriptive categories: disengagement, activity, and continuity theories; age stratification; minority group theory; life events and stress theory; and homogeneity *vs.* heterogeneity theory.

Disengagement, Activity, and Continuity Theories

Disengagement theory states that aging inevitably causes physical, psychological, and social disengagement (Cumming & Henry, 1961). Physical disengagement means a reduction in the amount of physical activity, a slowing down, and a conservation of energy. Psychological disengagement refers to the withdrawing of concern from the wider world to primary concern for people and things directly affecting oneself, a shifting of attention from the outer world to the inner world of one's own feelings and thoughts. It involves the reduction of mental and emotional energy. Social disengagement means the reduction of social activity and involvement, a "mutual withdrawal or disengagement between the aging person and others in the social system" (Cumming & Henry, 1961).

Two main parts of this theory have become most controversial. The first part states that most older people, independent of ill health or poverty, in fact do progressively disengage as they become older. The second part states that disengagement is *good* for both the aged and society. It is good for the aged because it is an acceptance of the inevitable decline and death, and the best way to adapt to the declining abilities of old age. Therefore, according to this theory, disengaged older people tend to be happier and healthier than those who try to remain more active. Disengagement is good for society because it can gradually transfer the functions previously performed by the aged to the young, and thus society can avoid the problems caused by increasing incompetence or sudden death of the aged.

Activity theory is the direct opposite of disengagement theory (Havighurst, 1963). Activity theory states that disengagement is not inevitable, except shortly before death, and many older people show little or no overall disengagement. Furthermore, it states that activity rather than disengagement is good for the individual and society. Activity maintains health, happiness, and longevity.

Continuity theory, as usually formulated, is not clearly different from either disengagement or activity theory (Neugarten, 1964; Atchley, 1972). Its main principle is that persons' life-long experiences creates in them predispositions which they will maintain if possible. However, whether a person disengages or remains active is determined by the complex interrelationships among predispositions, biological and psychological changes, and situational opportunities. For our purposes, the major hypothesis from continuity theory is that most older people tend to maintain similar attitudes, levels of function, and activities *relative to their age cohort*, despite overall age changes. This hypothesis is in contrast to the life events stress theory, which predicts marked changes in attitudes and activities when major life events take place.

We will see that the Duke Longitudinal Studies have evidence that support some aspects of all three theories. The chapters on retirement, social activities, social networks, sexual behavior, and life satisfaction are most relevant to these theories.

Age Stratification: Aging, Period, and Cohort Effects

Age stratification is a general conceptual model of life-span development, rather than a theory about aging with testable propositions (Riley, Johnson, & Foner, 1972). The basic idea in this model is the usefulness of viewing society as composed of layers (strata) of age groups, just as it can be viewed as composed of strata of social classes or racial groups. At any one point in time, these strata are composed of different age groups with different roles and the different expectations, facilities, rewards, or deprivations that define those roles. As time goes on, these age groups known as *birth cohorts* move up in the age-stratification system, both responding to the system and shaping it as they move through. At the same time, historical (environmental) changes are also molding the system and the birth cohorts within it.

One implication of this model is that age strata have differential access to facilities and the good things in life—just as the socioeconomic strata do. The degree to which this is true among the aged will be explored in the chapter on socioeconomic status.

Another implication of this model is that it emphasizes the importance of distinguishing between age, period, and cohort effects. This is a difficult task methodologically, but theoretically it is clear that becoming older may have different effects from those of belonging to a particular birth cohort, and each of these may have different effects from those of living in a particular historical period. The issue here is whether observed differences between age groups is due to aging, or to the changing environment (period), or to birth-cohort differences that result from the unique historical experiences of the different cohorts.

The early, and still most common, method of studying aging is cross-sectional. In this method several different age groups are studied at one point in time and the differences between the age groups are usually assumed to reflect aging effects. The fallacy of this assumption is that cross-sectional age-group differences are composed of both aging effects and cohort differences. Therefore, observed age-group differences in a cross-sectional study may be all or partly the result of cohort differences rather than aging effects, and a cross-sectional study cannot distinguish between these two effects. For example, we now know that much of the lower intellectual abilities of older persons are due to cohort differences rather than to aging effects.

Because of this problem, longitudinal studies have become more common. In this method one or more birth cohorts are repeatedly studied over time, in order to reveal changes within the individuals as they age. The difficulty with this method is that longitudinal differences over time are composed of both aging effects and period effects (changes in the environment over time). Therefore, observed longitudinal differences may be all or partly the result of changes in the environment rather than aging effects.

A solution is the use of cross-sequential designs, which is a combination of cross-sectional and longitudinal methods (Palmore, 1978a). In a cross-sequential design, two or more birth cohorts are measured two or more times, and the interval between measurements equals the number of years in the age cohorts. This makes possible the comparison of three kinds of differences: cross-sectional (which controls for period effects), longitudinal (which controls for cohorts effects), and time-lag (which controls for aging effects). From the comparison of these three differences it is possible to separate and estimate age, period, and cohort effects (see Methods of Analysis section). The second longitudinal study was designed as a cross-sequential study and the cross-sequential method of analysis will be used to separate age, period, and cohort effects when possible. For some purposes, data from the first longitudinal study will also be analyzed using this method, although it was not designed as a cross-sequential study.

Minority Group Theory

This theory is somewhat similar to the age-stratification model, but draws its concepts and principles from race and ethnic group theory. It asserts that the aged are a minority group in many of the same ways that blacks, Indians, and women are minority groups (Palmore, 1978b). It asserts that most people in our society (including many of the aged themselves) are prejudiced against the aged, believing that the majority of the aged are sick or disabled, senile, hopeless, useless, ugly, unpleasant, unwanted, poor, and miserable. The fact that all these stereotypes are generally false does not prevent them from being believed by most persons, even educated persons, in our society (Palmore, 1977).

A second proposition is that because of such beliefs there is wide-spread conscious and unconscious discrimination against the aged, especially in employment, but also in the general community and even in families. Because of this discrimination, the aged suffer from unnecessary economic deprivation, segregation, and loss of roles and status. This proposition will be examined in the chapters on retirement, socioeconomic status, and social networks.

Life Events and Stress

Life events theory maintains that major events in later life such as retirement, widowhood, children leaving home, or moving, produce stresses which result in physical and/or mental illness (Dohrenwend & Dohrenwend, 1974). Furthermore, these events tend to have additive effects so that persons with more such events are more likely to develop physical and mental illness. Other theories of stress assert that the outcome (such as illness) of such potential stressors depends on a complex set of intervening variables such as personal resources, the social situation, coping styles, and defenses (House, 1974). Evidence on how stressful these events are and the factors related to better or worse adaptation to them will be discussed primarily in the chapters on retirement, social networks, and life satisfaction.

Homogeneity vs. Heterogeneity

This issue is whether individuals become more like each other or more different from each other as they age. It is clear that differentiation generally increases with age in the early years, but it is unclear whether this is true in the middle and late years of life (Maddox & Douglas, 1974).

A number of life-span developmentalists theorize that individual differences observed in the middle years are accentuated in late life. They theorize that this increasing heterogeneity may be due to a weakening of social constraints that allows individual preferences to flourish, or to the aging declines in some persons contrasted with maintenance or improvement in function in other persons.

In contrast, proponents of the homogeneity theory argue that aging persons become more like each other because death is the common end point of life and as individuals approach death they decline to a lower common denominator. Increased morbidity limits the functioning of aging individuals and thus narrows the range and dispersion of performance.

Another version of this controversy is whether men and women become increasingly different, remain the same, or become more like the other group. Neugarten (1964) has asserted that the "sexes become increasingly divergent with age" while Cameron (1968) has found converging interests between aged men and women.

One reason such controversies remain is that longitudinal data are necessary to answer them. Data from our longitudinal studies on this issue will be presented in the chapters on socioeconomic status, social activities, social networks, sexual behavior, and life satisfaction.

The Duke Longitudinal Studies

A primary purpose of the Duke Longitudinal Studies was to measure changes in the same individuals as they age and thereby compensate for the weaknesses of cross-sectional studies. It was recognized that this was the only way to directly study aging *processes* as distinct from age-cohort differences. In addition, it was recognized that longitudinal studies have several other advantages; antecedents can be distinguished from consequences, consistent trends can be distinguished from temporary fluctuations, retrospective distortion is minimized, early warning signs of disease or death can be studied, predictors of longevity or other outcomes can be studied, and effects of one change on another kind of change can be studied.

Another feature of the Duke Longitudinal Studies is that they are multidisciplinary. The investigator team has included internists, immunologists, opthalmologists, radiologists, dermatologists, psychiatrists, psychologists, sociologists, and social workers. While this book focuses on social patterns, we will frequently show the relationship of social factors to other factors with data developed by other members of the team.

The next two sections describe the objectives and designs of the two longitudinal studies of aging that provide the data for the findings to be presented.

The First Longitudinal Study

Objectives. The first longitudinal study of aging was officially designated as a study of "the effect of aging upon the nervous system, a physiological, psychological, and sociological study of aging." Beginning in 1950, preliminary investigation and pilot studies were initiated with the objectives of determining if a longitudinal study was practical, feasible, and of value. Until this time most of the studies of the aging processes had been carried out utilizing patients for subjects who were institutionalized, receiving medical services, and/or assistance from social agencies. The decision was made to investigate the processes of aging among a panel of noninstitutionalized males and females, 60 years of age and over, from the time of initial observation to death. This study was conceived as exploratory and interdisciplinary. Its organization was intended to facilitate the accumulation of the widest possible range of observations from investigators with a variety of theoretical perspectives on elderly subjects residing in the community. The study was not guided by any single theory of aging. The focus has been on hypothesis generation and testing, reflecting the variety of investigators who have brought different theoretical perspectives to their analysis of the data. The project has therefore

Table 1-1. *Participants in the first longitudinal study by round.*

Round #	Dates	Total participants	No. having physical exams	No. having psychological exams	No. furnishing social data
1	3/55–5/61*	270	268	267	268
2	9/59–5/61	183	181	182	182
3	1/64–3/65	178	138	140	172
4	10/66–6/67	138	109	110	136
5	4/68–1/69	110	92	93	107
6	2/70–8/70	108	94	92	101
7	1/72–5/72	81	65	60	74
8	2/73–8/73	68	62	57	54
9	4/74–9/74	57	55	52	55
10	12/74–8/75	56	53	47	51
11	3/76–8/76	44	42	41	41

* Ten of the participants in the first round had their first examinations after the second round of examinations had started for other participants.

offered each investigator an opportunity for contact with colleagues with different theoretical interests and perspectives, and an opportunity for the use of the data of other investigators as control variables in their own research undertakings.

In both the first and second longitudinal studies, the emphasis has been on *normal* processes of aging. *Normal* can mean either *healthy* or *typical*. The longitudinal studies encompass both meanings: they studied *typical* aging processes among relatively *healthy* community residents. Also both studies have emphasized the physical, psychological, *and* social processes of aging and their interrelationships in order to develop a comprehensive understanding of the total process.

The first longitudinal study, however, because of its twenty-one year span is uniquely suited for the analysis of predictors of longevity and of factors related to maintenance of function over long periods of time.

Design. The study began in 1955 with a panel of noninstitutionalized persons aged 60 to 94 and includes eleven observations of panelists over a period of twenty-one years. Relatively complete information is available on 270 persons, 260 of whom were in the first round of observations and 10 of whom were added in the second round but whose initial data were coded as in the first round. Survivors were examined periodically, and the time between examinations decreased as the research progressed. For example, approximately 36 months separated the first and second examinations and approximately 12 months separated examination 10 and 11. The 11th and final examination on 44 persons was made in 1976 (Table 1-1). This table also shows the number of persons in each round with physical examinations, psychological examinations, and social examinations. The total number of participants is greater than the number in any one type of examination because some had one type but not another type.

The panelists, who were recruited to participate in periodic, intensive two-day examinations, were selected from a pool of volunteers so as to insure that their age, sex, racial, and socioeconomic characteristics would reflect the range and distribution of these characteristics in the community. Essential controls were therefore available for hypothesis testing.

The panel is adequate for testing a wide range of hypotheses relating different variables, as well as for evaluating hypotheses about changes in variables over time in the later years of life. The panel data are not, however, sufficient for generalizations about the distribution of characteristics or variables among older persons generally. Panelists at the first examination tended to have been of higher social status, in better health, and more active than older persons generally. This difference is commonly observed in all longitudinal studies of older persons and even in social surveys of older persons employing probability sampling procedures, because advantaged persons tend to be more likely than others to participate in such research studies (Maddox, 1962). The survivors examined in later rounds became an even more superior group than those in the first round. For further information on the study, see Palmore, 1970.

The Second Longitudinal Study

Objectives. As the first longitudinal study progressed, it became apparent that in order to fully understand variations in the aging processes, one needed to start earlier than at age 60 or 70. Therefore the second longitudinal study was begun as a supplement to the first study in three specific ways. It covered younger ages (46-70), those often referred to as "middle age." Its focus was on patterns of adaptation to the normal stresses of middle age such as widowhood, retirement, and changes in living arrangement. Thirdly, it was designed to allow cross-sequential types of analysis in order to partial out the effects of aging from differences between periods of measurement. Thus, it shared with the first study an interest in normal processes of physical, psychological, and social aging, but was distinguished by its emphasis on adaptation to normal stresses of middle age, and by its cross-sequential design.

Design. The second study began in 1968 with a stratified random sample of 502 persons aged 45-69 at the time of sampling, drawn primarily from the membership list of the major health insurance association in the area (Table 1-2). This list included the majority of the middle- and upper-income residents of Durham County under age 65. Because few persons over age 65 belong to the association, the sample of members aged 65-69 was supplemented by a sample of 32 persons who had been patients at the Duke Medical Center. This resulted in the 65-69 sample being somewhat above the average of the rest of the panelists in terms of socioeconomic status. Illiterate persons were excluded from the study because they could not take the written tests. Institutionalized or homebound persons were excluded because they could not come in for the examinations. Blacks were excluded because they were being studied separately in another project.

Within each of ten age-sex categories, names were randomly drawn from the list and contacted for examinations until quotas in each category were filled. The quotas were designed to allow about 40 persons to be retested in each of the cohorts at the end of six years, assuming a 10 percent dropout rate and the age-sex specific mortality rates. Because the study required eight hours of examinations without compensation, about half of the persons contacted refused to participate.

Table 1-2. *Participants in the second longitudinal study by round.*

Round #	Dates	Total participants	No. having physical exams	No. having psychological exams	No. furnishing social data
1	8/68– 4/70	502	502	502	502
2	8/70– 3/72	443	438	438	443
3	6/72– 7/74	386	384	383	383
4	8/74–10/76	375	374	375	375

Table 1-3. *Characteristics of participants compared with nonparticipants.*

Characteristic	Participants	Nonparticipants
Median years of school completed	12.5	12.3
Percent married	85%	85%
Mean health rating (4-point scale)	2.2	2.1
Percent with private physician	90%	76%

Note.—Participants = 502; nonparticipants = 94.

In order to estimate how our sample might differ from the other members of the health association, we compared our sample with a sample of those who refused to participate (using information from a telephone survey of nonparticipants). This comparison showed that the participants were quite similar to the nonparticipants on education, marital status, and health rating (Table 1-3). Fourteen percent more of the participants reported that they had a private physician, but this could have been caused by the fact that the participants were encouraged to report the name of a "private physician" to whom a report of the medical examination could be sent.

In order to estimate how our sample might differ from the U.S. population, we compared our sample with all white persons in the U.S. aged 45-69 (using 1970 census statistics). Our sample had somewhat more married, employed, better educated, and in the upper-level occupations (Table 1-4). The comparisons indicate that our sample was fairly similar in these characteristics to the other members of the health association, but tended to be somewhat above average for all white Americans in this age range. Also, our sample was limited to residents of the Durham area. Therefore, any generalizations from this study should be made with caution and with recognition of its above average nature.

Survivors of the original sample were reexamined every two years until the fourth and final round in 1974-1976, which included 375 examinations. Survivors in this study also were an even more superior group than those at the beginning of the study. For further information on the study, see Palmore, 1974.

Table 1-4. *Characteristics of study sample compared with U.S. white persons aged 45-69.*

Characteristic	Study sample	U.S. white 45-69
Percent married	85%	79%
Percent employed	66%	59%
Median years of school completed	12.5	11.1
Percent professional or managers	35%	25%

Methods of Analysis

In addition to the usual methods of cross-tabulations, comparisons of means between groups, correlation and regression analysis, there are some special methods that are particularly useful for the analysis of longitudinal data. The following are special methods used in this monograph to analyze data from our longitudinal studies: (*a*) age, period, and cohort analysis; (*b*) change graphs; (*c*) residual change analysis; and (*d*) longevity difference.

Age, Period, and Cohort Analysis

We earlier pointed out that a cross-sequential design was necessary to separate out the effects of age, period, and cohort. The method we use for this has been described in detail previously (Palmore, 1978a), but we will summarize the essential steps here. First, the data must be arranged so that the time interval between times of measurement must equal the number of years in each birth cohort. Second, each of the three types of differences must be measured: longitudinal (difference between earlier and later measurements on the same cohort), cross-sectional difference between cohorts at the same point in time), and time-lag (difference between earlier measurement on an older cohort and later measurement on a younger cohort). Third, inference about the effects contained in these differences are based on the fact that each difference is composed of two effects: longitudinal difference equals age plus period; cross-sectional difference equals age plus cohort; and time-lag difference equals period minus cohort. If there are no significant differences it is usually safe to infer that there are no age, period, nor cohort effects.

If there are two significant differences, it is usually safe to assume that there is one and only one of the three effects present: the one which is common to the two significant differences. If there are three significant differences, there may be two unequal effects present or three effects present, and outside evidence or theory is necessary to distinguish these two possibilities.

Finally, the theoretical causes of any inferred effects need to be determined. Age effects may be due to biological, psychological, and/or social-role changes with age. Period effects may be due to changes in the environment, measurements, and/or practice. Cohort effects may be due to genetic shifts and/or the interaction of specific historical situations with the cohorts at specific ages.

There are other methods that can be used to separate age, period, and cohort effects under certain conditions or with certain assumptions, but the above method will be used in this monograph because it is more flexible and involves fewer assumptions than the other methods.

It should be clear that we are not using *cause* in the sense of a necessary or sufficient cause, but in the general sense of "any event, circumstance, or condition that brings about or helps bring about a result" (*Webster's New Collegiate Dictionary*). Similarly, in using *effect* we do not distinguish between immediate and long-term outcomes; but are using the word in the general sense of a "condition or occurrence traceable to a cause." Finally, *time* refers to the "period during which an action, process, or condition exists or continues."

Change Graphs

In order to graphically depict longitudinal changes in our panelists two types of composite graphs will be presented. Longitudinal changes in the first longitudinal study will be shown by a series of lines connecting mean scores or percentages on pairs of examinations for all the persons present for both examinations. For example, Figure 3-1 presents the percentage not employed, by sex and mean year of examination, for each pair of rounds in the first six rounds of the first longitudinal study. Thus the first solid line on the left of the graph indicates that among men present at rounds 1 and 2, 53 percent were not employed in the first round, and this increased to 55 percent in the second round. The next solid line shows that this percentage increased from 50 in round 2 to 65 in round 3. The lines do not usually connect with each other because some die or drop out at each round, which slightly changes the composition of the group present for each pair of rounds.

In the second longitudinal study, a similar graph is used except that each line connects the mean scores or percentages in the first round with the last round for the persons in a given age cohort. These lines do not usually connect with each other because sampling variation makes the individual cohorts somewhat different from each other. However, the slope of the lines represents true longitudinal changes in each cohort, even though the absolute differences between cohorts are unimportant. For example, the first solid line in Figure 3-2 shows that among men in the first cohort the percentage retired increased from 2 percent in the first round to 10 percent in the last round; the second solid line shows that the percentage increased from zero to 17 among the men in the second cohort; etc. It should be understood that the validity of inferring age changes from such graphs depends on two assumptions: that there are no significant period effects on the changes analyzed, and that the samples from each cohort are comparable in terms of the changes analyzed. All the data presented in these graphs have been carefully examined and appear to justify these assumptions. Data that did not appear to justify these assumptions are not presented in this manner.

Residual Change Analysis

A major problem in longitudinal analysis is the best way to measure individual changes with aging. A number of statisticians have pointed out the problems of using simple change scores, i.e., the difference between an earlier and later score (Cronback & Furby, 1970). One of these problems is the "regression to the mean" effect: persons with higher scores will tend to have more downward changes and persons with lower scores will tend to have more upward changes. A second problem with using change scores is that any errors in the measure get doubled in a change score because there are two adminstrations of the measure involved.

A solution to both of these problems is the method of residual change analysis. In this method a regression analysis is performed in which the score on the second administration of the measure is the dependent variable, and the score on the first administration is the first independent variable. This has the effect of controlling for initial level, thus eliminating the effects of regression to the mean, as well as reducing the measurement error caused by the doubling of errors in a change score. Second and subsequent variables introduced in the regression equation then are related only to the residual change in the measure, because initial level has been controlled. (Palmore et al., 1979).

Longevity Difference

In our previous analyses of longevity we have used two alternate measures, the Longevity Index (LI) and the Longevity Quotient (LQ). The LI is simply the number of years a panelist survived after initial testing or, for a living person, an estimate of the number of years he/she will have lived after initial testing, based on life expectancy tables (Palmore, 1971a). The LQ is the LI divided by the expected number of years to be survived after initial examination, thus controlling for age, sex, and race differences in longevity.

We have now developed a third measure which is used in this monograph: the Longevity Difference (LD). The LD is the number of years actually survived after initial testing, minus the life expectancy based on age, sex, and race of the participant. This controls for age, sex, and race differences, as does the LQ, but it has the advantage of being directly interpretable as the number of years survived in addition to (or less than) the expected number of years. For example, if a white male was 65 at initial testing, his life expectancy would have been 13.1 more years. If he actually lived 18.1 years, his LD would be +5 (18.1−13.1) meaning that he lived 5 years more than expected. On the other hand, if he lived only 10.1 years, his LD would be −3, meaning that he lived 3 years less than expected.

Summary

The two purposes of this book are to review previous theories and findings on social patterns in normal aging, and to present the findings from the Duke Longitudinal Studies in Aging. The major issues dealt with are disengagement, activity, and continuity theories; age stratification; minority group theory; life events and stress; and homogeneity vs. heterogeneity.

Although most previous studies of aging have been cross-sectional, and, therefore, do not directly study the processes of aging, the Duke Studies employ a cross-*sequential* design, which combines cross-sectional and longitudinal methods and makes it possible to separate and estimate age, period, and cohort effects. Other features of the Duke Studies are their multidisciplinary nature, their focus on normal aging, and their use of change graphs, residual change analysis, and longevity difference analysis. They were begun in 1955 with the first longitudinal study, which contained a panel of 267 noninstitutionalized persons aged 60 to 94, and this study was continued for 21 years. Although the panel was not a probability sample, it was adequate for testing a wide range of hypotheses relating different variables and for detecting changes in variables over time. The second longitudinal study, designed to allow cross-sequential types of analysis, began in 1968 with a stratified random sample of 502 persons aged 45-69, and this study was continued for 8 years. Survivors of the original sample were reexamined every two years until the fourth and final round in 1974-1976, which included 375 examinations. Both studies attempted to gather comprehensive data on physical, psychological, *and* social processes of aging.

Most chapters of this book are divided into three main sections: aging effects, antecedents, and consequences of the subject of the chapter. Each of these sections first discusses previous theories and finding, and then discusses the relevant findings from the Duke Longitudinal Studies. Each chapter closes with a summary. A final chapter reviews our conclusions relevant to the major theoretical issues and discusses implications of our conclusions.

Chapter 2. Socioeconomic Status

We begin with socioeconomic status because it has such profound implications for most other aspects of aging. Socioeconomic status (SES) refers to a person's relative rank in our stratification system and is usually measured by a person's education, occupation, and financial status. SES determines whether one lives in luxury or in poverty; whether one is financially secure or is continually worrying about getting enough food, shelter, and clothing; whether one has the education and training to function well in the modern world; whether one has (or had) an interesting and prestigious occupation; whether one can afford adequate diet and medical care to maintain good health. In short, SES determines to a large extent one's access to many, if not most, of the good things in life. This is usually as true of old age as it is of younger ages.

Aging Effects

Previous Research

Max Weber (1947) distinguished between two dimensions of socioeconomic status: class (*Klasse*) and prestige (*Standische Lage*). Class refers to the probability of having goods, services, and a beneficial environment. In our society this is best indicated by income. Prestige is based on mode of living, education, occupation, or prestige of birth. In our society prestige is best indicated by education and occupation.

Education. Aged persons tend to have less education than younger ones. For example, 63 percent of those 65 and over never graduated from high school, compared with only 26 percent of those 18 to 64 (Harris, 1975). But clearly, this is not an aging effect; older people do not lose their education as they grow older. This is a classic example of a pure cohort effect: each younger cohort has received more education than the previous one. As a matter of fact, some aged acquire *more* education as they grow older; 5 percent of those aged 55-64 and 2 percent of those 65 and over were enrolled in courses in 1974 (Harris, 1975). Thus, the effect of aging on education is to slightly increase the averages over the years, despite the fact that the aged generally have substantially lower levels of education than do younger persons. Furthermore, as time goes on and the more educated younger cohorts move into the aged category, the average educational level of the aged will substantially increase.

Occupation. Similarly the (present or former) occupational levels of the aged tend to be lower than those of younger persons. For example, in 1970 the occupation similarity index resulting from a comparison of those 65 and over with those aged 45-64 was 88, which means that 12 percent of the aged had occupations lower than 12 percent of the middle-aged (Palmore, 1976). But again, this is mostly a cohort effect rather than an aging effect; each younger cohort has more education and achieves higher occupational levels than the previous cohort. Although, there may be some decline in occupational levels among those who continue to work beyond age 65, this is not yet well documented.

Of more importance is the fact that most aged persons no longer have *any* occupation; only about 12 percent of persons over 65 are employed in any given week, and most of them are in part-time employment (Harris, 1975). And it is unclear how much prestige or status retired persons derive from their former occupations. Retired persons probably have higher status than unemployed workers, and persons retired from prestigious occupations probably maintain somewhat more prestige than those from lower occupations. But the salience of former occupations for the SES of retired persons is probably less than the salience of current occupation for those still employed. The more general problem is that retired persons tend to suffer a decline in status both because they are no longer productive and because they are old. We are still a predominantly work-oriented and youth-oriented society. This is one manifestation of the ageism that is widespread in our society (Palmore, 1979).

Financial status. There is more poverty among the aged, and older persons have lower average incomes than younger adults. In 1975, 14 percent of persons 65 and over had incomes below the federal poverty levels, compared to 12 percent for persons under 65 (Administration on Aging, 1978). Also, persons over 65 had mean incomes that were about half as much as those aged 55–64.

Here we have a combination of aging effects and cohort effects. The aged usually do suffer some decline in income as they age, especially upon retirement. The Cornell Study of Retirement estimated that the average retired person's income declined to 56 percent of preretirement income (Streib & Schneider, 1971). However, part of the difference in incomes between old and young is a cohort difference: the younger cohorts have more education, higher occupations, and so earn more income throughout their lives than did the aged. One estimate based on the cohort aged 65–74 in 1960 found only a 15 percent decline in constant dollar income after age 65 (Miller, 1965).

Furthermore, there are several factors that offset the decline in money income among the aged. First, there are the many tax advantages that the aged enjoy because of their age, including reductions in property tax, double personal exemptions on income tax, and tax exempt income such as Social Security benefits (Schultz, 1976). It has been estimated that the aged save about $3.5 billion a year through federal income tax provisions (Surrey, 1973). Second, there are substantial transfer payments to the aged such as Medicare benefits and housing subsidies which do not show as income. In fact, it has been estimated that when tax advantages and transfer payments are taken into account, the aged actually receive *more* of the nation's personal income (14 percent) than their proportion in the population (10 percent) (Fried et al., 1973). Part of this is because there are a substantial number of rich aged who inflate the total proportion of income received by the aged (the majority of millionaires are over age 60: Binstock & Shanas, 1976); and part is because the proportion of the population under age 65 includes children who usually have no income.

Third, persons in their 60s tend to have more assets than younger persons, such as equity in their home, savings, and investments (Henretta & Campbell, 1978). These assets can be used to meet emergencies and maintain a standard of living above what could be afforded from current income alone. Fourth, income needs usually decline as child support and work-related expenses decline.

Because of these offsetting factors, *adequacy* of income often declines little or none (Streib & Schneider, 1971). All of this is not to deny that there is a substantial proportion of the aged (about 15 to 25 percent) who are in poverty or severe financial difficulties. It *does* deny the widespread belief (even reflected in the leading text, Atchley, 1977, p. 125) that "most older people are relatively poor."

In summary, previous research indicates that although the aged have less education, their level of education tends to increase slightly as they age; although few aged continue to have occupations, they tend to maintain some status from their former occupations; and although most aged suffer substantial reductions in income upon retirement, offsetting factors tend to reduce the impact of this reduction on their standard of living.

Findings from the Duke Longitudinal Studies

Education. The average number of years of education completed in the second longitudinal study (ages 45-70) was twelve (the equivalent of graduation from high school), and the youngest cohort had about one more year of education on the average than the next two older cohorts, which illustrates the cohort effect of more education in the younger cohorts. However, the oldest cohort (ages 64-70) had about a year more education than would be expected. This shows that the 65 and over sample was somewhat above the average of the other panelists because of the special sample supplementation in this cohort (described in chapter 1).

The first longitudinal study participants (aged 60-94) had completed ten years of education on the average, but those over 80 had about one year less education than those in the younger cohorts. This again illustrates the cohort effect of older cohorts having less education.

Occupation. The second longitudinal study panelists were distributed fairly evenly among the three major categories of professionals and managers, clerical and technicians, and manual workers. There were no substantial departures from this pattern by age group, except that the 64 and over group had substantially more in the professional and manager category, which again shows that they are above the averages of the other age groups (Table 2-1).

The first longitudinal study panelists had about equal proportions in the professional category and the manual worker category, but substantially less in the clerical and technical category (Table 2-2). There were no substantial departures from this pattern by age group, except that those 80 and over had somewhat more than expected in the professional-manager category.

Financial status. Total income of the panelist and spouse was asked at each round of the Adaptation Study, so we could do an age, period, and cohort effects analysis (Table 2-3). The mean incomes for round 4 have been adjusted by the consumer price index (reduced by .32) so that they approximate the dollar value of

Table 2-1. *Occupational distribution by age as reported in the second longitudinal study.*

Age	N	Professionals and managers	Clerical and technical	Manual	None
46-51	98	30%	28%	42%	1%
52-57	128	29	26	45	1
58-63	112	33	27	37	4
64+	160	44	21	32	3
Total	498	35	25	38	2

Table 2-2. *Occupational distribution by age as reported in the first longitudinal study.*

Age	N	Professionals and managers	Clerical and technical	Manual	None
60-69	127	45%	11%	43%	1
70-79	109	39	11	49	1
80+	34	50	12	38	0
Total	270	43	11	45	1

the 1968-70 wave. Thus, for the purpose of this analysis we can assume little or no period effect. This means that the longitudinal differences between 1968-70 and 1974-76 can be attributed to aging effects. Looking across the rows we see that each cohort has had some decline in income over the six-year period, from 2 percent in the youngest cohort to a peak decline of 23 percent in the third cohort (aged 58-63 at first interview). This indicates that income decline with age is minimal in the early 50s, is greatest in the mid-60s (the usual retirement age), and is less in the 70s (Table 2-3).

It may be noted that the fourth cohort had more income in 1968-1970 than the third cohort did in 1974-1976, even though both groups were aged 64-70 at those times. This is probably explained by the higher than average SES of the fourth cohort because of the special sample supplementation in this cohort.

If we add together all four declines over the six-year interval, the total is 50 percent. This would indicate that over the 24 years between the late 40s and early 70s the average person's income declined by about one-half (in constant dollars). This estimate is similar to others described in the previous research section.

Since we can assume little or no period effect, we attribute the time-lag differences to cohort effects. Time-lag differences are those between an older cohort at the earlier measurement and the younger cohort at the later measurement (when the younger cohort has become the same age as the older cohort was at the earlier measurement). For example, the mean income of the youngest cohort in 1974-1976 (when it was aged 52-57) was $12,954, compared to $12,327 for the second cohort in

Table 2-3. *Mean income by age,* period, and cohort.*

Cohort	N**	1968-1970	1974-1976 (adjusted to 1969 $)	% decline
1	80	$13,231 (age 46-51)	$12,954 (age 52-57)	2%
2	99	12,327 (age 52-57)	11,151 (age 58-63)	10%
3	86	10,244 (age 58-63)	7,907 (age 64-70)	23%
4	103	8,960 (age 64-70)	7,628 (age 71-76)	15%
Total	368	11,094 (age 46-70)	9,799 (age 52-76)	12%

* Age of cohort at time of interview given in parenthesis under mean income. Income includes spouse's income.
** Includes only those returning for 1974-1976 interview.
Source. Second longitudinal study.

1968-1970 (when it was also aged 52-57). This shows a $627 difference in income between the first and second cohorts (at the same ages). Similarly, there is a $907 time-lag difference between the second and third cohorts. These time-lag differences show that later cohorts had higher incomes than earlier cohorts when ages are matched. The difference between the third and fourth cohorts is misleading due to the above average nature of the 65–70-year-old sample described above.

Note that the cohort effects and the aging effects add together to equal the cross-sectional differences observed between age/cohort groups by looking down the columns in Table 2-3. Such cross-sectional differences are often erroneously attributed entirely to aging effects. This analysis shows that a substantial part of the cross-sectional difference in income is due to cohort effects.

We also asked panelists in the first interview to estimate their total income five years ago. Although such retrospective estimates are known to be less accurate than current estimates, the results support the patterns shown by the above analysis. After adjusting for inflation, the first cohort's income showed a 5 percent increase from five years ago; the second showed a 3 percent decline from five years ago (corresponding with the 2 percent decline shown by current estimates for this age range); the third showed a 7 percent decline (compared to the 10 percent decline in current estimates); and the fourth showed a 29 percent decline (compared to the 23 percent decline in current estimates). Thus, both current and retrospective estimates show the same pattern of increasing declines with age through the mid-60s.

As a result of the income declines, the standard deviation also declined by about $2,300 in all cohorts. Thus, these individuals became more homogeneous in terms of real income.

In the first longitudinal study we did not ask for amount of income, but we did ask, "Are you in a better or worse financial position now than you were at age 55?" Table 2-4 shows that the most frequent response (44 percent) was "Better now." Thus almost half of the panelists thought that any declines in income had been

Table 2-4. *Present financial position compared to age 55 by age group.*

Age	N	Worse now	Same	Better now
60-69	125	28%	28%	44%
70-79	105	32	17	42
80+	31	35	19	45
Total	261	34	22	44

Source. First longitudinal study.

Table 2-5. *Mean economic security by age,* period, and cohort.*

Cohort	N**	1955-59	1966-67
1	66	3.8 (60-69)	4.1 (70-79)
2	43	3.3 (70-79)	3.7 (80-89)
Total	109	3.6 (60-79)	3.9 (70-89)

* Approximate ages indicated in parenthesis.
** Includes only those returning for 1965-67 interview.

Source. First longitudinal study.

more than offset by reduced expenses, lower taxes, etc. In addition, about one-fifth thought they were in about the same financial position. This finding supports the conclusion in the review of previous research that *adequacy* of income often declines little or none (despite substantial declines in *actual* income).

Furthermore, there appears to be little or no trend with age in the proportions. Thus it appears that, regardless of age, only a minority of elders in our study experienced a substantial decline in the adequacy of their income. The Cornell Study of Retirement found similar proportions who said their income in retirement "was not enough" (Streib & Schneider, 1971).

The first longitudinal study also included an economic security scale, which could range from 0 indicating least economic security, to 6 for maximum economic security (See Appendix A for details). An age, period, and cohort analysis indicates first, that both cohorts experienced slight *increases* in economic security over the first 10 years of the study (Table 2-5)—these increases may have been period effects due to increased social security and other benefits; it seems unlikely that they were aging effects—and second, the older cohort had somewhat lower economic security scores at both the beginning and end of the ten-year period. This appears to be the cohort effect we have seen before, with older cohorts having less income and assets than younger cohorts.

Subjective status. Another standard dimension of socioeconomic status is the subjective dimension, the class with which the individual identifies and how much respect or prestige the individual thinks he/she has. But there has been little or no

Table 2-6. *Subjective class identification by age group.*

Age	N	Upper and upper-middle	Middle	Working and lower
46-51	98	20%	47%	33%
52-57	128	25	40	35
58-63	112	25	42	33
64+	160	29	52	19
Total	498	25	46	29

Source. Second longitudinal study.

Table 2-7. *Mean score on the variable respected by age,* period, and cohort.*

Cohort	N**	1968-70	1974-76
1	80	5.9 (46-51)	5.9 (52-57)
2	100	5.9 (52-57)	5.9 (58-63)
3	88	5.9 (58-63)	6.0 (64-70)
4	106	5.7 (64-70)	5.8 (71-76)
Total	374	5.9 (46-70)	5.9 (52-76)

* Age given in parenthesis.
** Includes only those returning for 1974-76 interview.
Source. Second longitudinal study.

research on this dimension among elders. One might speculate that there would be a decline in subjective SES with age along with the declines in income and occupation.

The second longitudinal study contains two items dealing with subjective SES. The first question asked the panelists, "Which of the following descriptions best fit you? Upper class, upper-middle class, middle class, working class, or lower class?" There were few (2 percent) "upper class" responses, so these were combined with the "upper-middle class" responses for analysis. There was only one "lower class" response and it was combined with "working class." Almost half responded "middle class" and the other half split almost equally between the "upper middle" and the "working" class responses (Table 2-6). There do not seem to be any trends in class identification by age except that there are substantially less in the "working" category for the 64 and over group (because they are generally above average SES). This certainly provides no support for the idea of declining subjective SES with age. It is unfortunate, however, that this question was not repeated, so a longitudinal analysis is not possible.

Nevertheless, each panelist at each interview did rate how "respected" he/she appeared to be (seven-point scale). An age, period, and cohort analysis of these ratings shows almost no change over time and almost no differences between the cohorts (Table 2-7). This indicates that there were no age, period, or cohort effects,

Table 2-8. *Feelings of status by age,* period, and cohort.*

Cohort	N**	1955-59	1966-67
1	66	5.6 (60-69)	5.8 (70-79)
2	43	5.0 (70-79)	5.6 (80-89)
Total	109	5.4 (60-79)	5.7 (70-89)

* Age indicated in parenthesis.
** Includes only those returning for 1966-67 interview.
Source. First longitudinal study.

i.e., that panelists did not feel less respect as they aged, nor were there differences between cohorts or between year of interview in feelings of respect.

Panelists in the first longitudinal study were rated at each interview on a ten-point scale of "status or feeling of importance." An age, period, and cohort analysis shows that there were small increases in feelings of status over the ten-year period in both cohorts, with the older cohort showing a greater increase (Table 2-8). This indicates that the panelists felt growing respect and status as they aged, especially in the cohort moving into their 80s. However, the older cohort started with a lower rating. This complex pattern is difficult to interpret, but it does not seem to support the idea of any decline in subjective SES.

In summary, there is no evidence from either longitudinal study of any decline in subjective SES. Apparently most of these panelists managed to maintain their feelings of status and respect, despite declines in income and occupational involvement.

Factors Affecting Socioeconomic Status

Previous Research

Income. There is a large body of research which examines the factors affecting the income and occupations of those under age 65. This research has resulted in fairly standard theoretical models which are able to explain a large portion of the variation in later income or occupation by characteristics of family of origin and early attainments such as education. However, there has been only one application of these models to income of persons over age 65 (Henretta & Campbell, 1976).

Henretta and Campbell found that the factors determining income for males aged 66-77 were the same ones that determined income at earlier ages. The pattern of effects, and even the estimates of dollar effects, were quite similar before and after age 65. The most important factor was the person's former occupation, followed closely by his education. This was expected since income, occupation, and education are closely linked at earlier ages. Being married and the wife's having higher education were next in importance. Married males apparently have higher incomes because married persons need more income, unmarried persons may be discriminated against in salary, and perhaps unmarried persons have other characteristics which limit their earning capacity. The effect of the wife's higher education is apparently indirect through her life-long ability to contribute more to family income. Father's education comes next and apparently shows the advantage of coming from a higher SES family. The number of children is negatively related to income, possibly because more children deplete savings and possibly because higher income persons tend to restrict the number of their children. Father's occupation and respondent's age had little effect within this restricted age range. The entire set of eight factors was able to explain almost a third of the variance in income, which was even more than the variance explained at 55-64. Thus, even though retirement and aging reduce income substantially, the reduction apparently applies fairly uniformly across the range of SES and does not reduce the effects of previous factors determining income.

However, it should be noted that whether one is employed was not included in this model. Other evidence indicates that this becomes a most important factor determining income in old age. For example, persons over 65 working year round at full-time jobs have incomes more than twice as high as other aged (U.S. Census, 1974).

Assets. A second analysis by Henretta and Campbell recently found that financial assets (net worth) among persons aged 50 to 64 were determined in similar ways to their income (1978). In addition to the strong influence of earnings, other factors had strong negative influences on assets such as having little education, being unmarried, having large households, and having a lower occupation.

They also found that net worth increased between ages 55 to 64 at about 3 percent per year. They argue that since income and employment begin to decline during this period, assets become an increasingly important dimension of socioeconomic status among the aged. On the other hand, most of the assets of a majority of the aged are tied up as equity in an owned home (Schultz, 1976).

Findings from the Duke Longitudinal Studies

The second study had enough information to partially replicate Henretta and Campbell's analysis of the factors determining income. (Wife's education was missing and we could not use marital status because all the men aged 60-70 happened to be married.) Table 2-9 shows the results of this partial replication. The first column gives the results for the reduced form of the equation which contains only the background variables of age, father's education, and father's occupation. The second column gives the results for the complete equation. These results are remarkably similar to those of Henretta and Campbell in that father's education was the strongest determinant among the background variables; that two-thirds of the effects of father's education are indirect through the respondent's characteristics; that father's occupation had nonsignificant effects (actually small negative effects, probably related to the grossness of our nine occupational categories); that respondent's occupation had the strongest effect of all variables in the final equation; that number of children had similar small negative effects; and that the corrected amount of variance explained was within four points of the previous

Table 2-9. *Reduced form and complete equation for income of men aged 60-70: Standardized coefficients (beta).*

Variable	1	2
Age	−.06	−.08
Father's education	.40	.13
Father's occupation	−.07	−.18
Respondent's education		.30
Respondent's occupation		.38
Number of children		−.08
R^2	.13	.42
R^2 corrected for *df*	.10	.33

Source. Second longitudinal study.

study's variance explained. One notable difference was that age had a stronger effect in our study than the previous one (−.08 compared to −.01). This stronger effect is probably related to the fact that our age range (60-70) covered the normal retirement years, while their age range (66-77) started after the normal retirement years.

This similarity of results shows that the model of income determinants derived from large national surveys can be replicated on small local samples. It also indicates that our sample is fairly representative of the rest of the nation, at least in regard to income determinants.

Effects of Socioeconomic Status

Previous Research

Socioeconomic status probably influences almost all aspects of life in our society. This review will concentrate on those aspects where the influence is strongest and best known.

Physical health. One of the most serious consequences of lower SES is poor health. It is well known that poorer people in general have poorer health. The same is true of older people. For example, persons aged 65-74 with poverty level incomes report two or three times as many restricted activity days and bed-disability days per person as those with average or better incomes (Riley et al., 1968). Similarly, over one-third of older persons with incomes under $3,000 report that poor health is a very serious problem for them, compared to about ten percent for those with incomes over $7,000 (Harris, 1975).

However, we do not know how much of the association between poverty and illness is because poverty causes illness, and how much is because illness causes poverty. Almost certainly each tends to cause the other. The implication is that reducing illness would reduce poverty, and reducing poverty would reduce illness.

Medical care. One reason poverty causes illness is that the poor get poorer medical care. For example, 18 percent of those over 65 with less than $3,000 income said that not enough medical care was a very serious problem for them, compared to only 1 percent of those with incomes over $15,000 (Harris, 1975).

The introduction of Medicare and Medicaid has helped increase access to medical care among the poor aged, but in addition to the remaining financial barriers, there are many other barriers that restrict poor people's access to quality medical care: ignorance and denial, preference for home remedies and lay treatment, transportation problems, and attitudes of health practitioners.

Longevity. Studies in the U.S. and in Great Britain have consistently found a strong association between SES and longevity (Riley & Foner, 1968; Palmore & Stone, 1973). For example, unskilled laborers had almost twice as high mortality rates as professionals in the U.S. This again is due to the interacting factors of poverty and poor health.

Mental health. Most studies agree that upper SES persons tend to have better mental health and less mental illness. This is true of older persons as well. Studies in Ohio, New York, and San Francisco, all found mental illness more prevalent among lower SES old persons (Palmore, 1973).

Here again, the association is clear, but the controversy remains over the explanation of the association. One explanation asserts that both lower status and mental illness are caused by some third factor, such as inferior heredity or chronic physical illness. An alternate explanation asserts that mental illness causes the lower status. The explanation favored by most social scientists is that the multiple stresses of lower status, such as inadequate diet, housing, medical care, and education, as well as family and community disorganization, all combine to increase the rate of mental breakdown (Lowenthal & Berkman, 1967). These are not mutually exclusive explanations and all probably have some validity. However, it seems certain that, regardless of the initial cause of mental illness, the stresses of lower status complicate treatment and recovery.

Cognitive function. There are many kinds of cognitive functions, ranging from simple word recognition to complex problem solving. Each of these functions may be measured in several different ways. However, regardless of the function or the method of measurement, the almost universal finding is that upper SES persons have better cognitive function than lower. This is true of the aged as well (Botwinick, 1977).

Once again the relative influence of nature *vs.* nurture is unclear. Both factors are undoubtedly important. Persons with lower innate *capacities* for cognitive functioning tend to remain in, or drop down to, lower SES levels. But also, persons starting in lower SES levels, regardless of innate capacities, do not have as much opportunity for the education and other experiences that develop higher cognitive functioning *abilities*. The relative importance of nurture may be greater among the aged who were raised in an era when class of origin was more important in determining educational and occupational opportunities than they are today.

Social activity. SES appears to make little or no difference in certain social activities among elders, but makes a big difference in others. Specifically, there is no noticeable difference between income or education groups in the frequency of contacts with friends and relatives (Harris, 1975, p. 169). Similarly, there are small differences between upper and lower income groups in the frequency with which they help out their children or grandchildren, except that the affluent more often give gifts and help out with money (Harris, 1975, p. 77). The affluent also give more advice about business and jobs, but this is balanced by less advice on bringing up children and running a home. Church and synagogue attendance is also similar across SES groups.

On the other hand, there are about three times as many of the higher income group as the lowest group doing volunteer work (Harris, 1975, p. 98). Also college graduates attend restaurants, movies, parks, sports events, libraries, live theatre, musical concerts, museums, and community or recreation centers much more frequently than do those who are not college graduates (Harris, 1975, p. 178).

Perhaps as a result of the more frequent volunteer work and attendance at public facilities, the upper SES groups report "loneliness" and "not enough friends" much less than lower SES groups (Harris, 1975, p. 130).

Social problems. As might be expected, poor elders have more problems in general than affluent elders. The following were reported as personally "very serious" problems much more frequently by poor than by affluent elders: fear of crime, not feeling needed, not enough to do to keep busy, not enough job opportunities, not enough friends, poor housing, and not enough clothing (Harris, 1975, p. 130). In fact, most of these problems were almost never reported as "very serious personally" by those in the $15,000 and over group.

Life satisfaction. Despite the saying that "money can't buy happiness," those with more money and education report substantially more life satisfaction. For example, life satisfaction scores are about one-third higher among those with $15,000 or more than those with under $3,000 (Harris, 1975, p. 160). Most other studies have found a substantial positive relationship between income and life satisfaction (Edwards & Klemmack, 1973; Spreitzer & Snyder, 1974). Studies using other measures of SES such as occupation and education also usually find strong associations between income and life satisfaction among elders (Kutner, 1956; Neugarten, Havighurst, & Tobin, 1961; Cutler, 1973).

Thus, despite anecdotes about misery among the rich and happiness among the poor, previous research generally agrees that higher SES contributes toward higher life satisfaction.

Findings from the Duke Longitudinal Studies

Relationship of SES to other variables. In general, the Duke Longitudinal Studies confirm the findings of previous studies on the relationship of SES to health, cognitive function, social activity, and life satisfaction (Tables 2-10 and 2-11). Both studies consistently show that the upper SES groups are healthier than the lower, regardless of how SES and health is measured. The second study also shows that the upper SES groups report substantialy fewer psychosomatic symptoms than the lower groups. Since frequency of psychosomatic symptoms is

Table 2-10. *Relation of socioeconomic status to health, intelligence, social activity, and satisfaction.**

SES measure	Physical function	Health self-rating	Psycho-somatic symptoms	Intelli-gence	Relatives & close friends	Church meetings	Non-church meetings	Social hours	Affect balance	Life satisfaction
Education										
0–11	8.0	6.4	5.0	81	9.5	3.5	0.8	8.0	0.5	6.9
12	8.1	6.9	3.9	101	9.1	3.5	2.0	10.4	1.4	7.2
13–15	8.2	6.9	3.7	112	9.0	3.5	2.5	10.9	1.6	7.2
16+	8.3	7.1	2.9	127	7.5	2.8	2.6	12.0	1.5	6.9
Probability	.05	.01	.01	.01	.01	ns	.01	.01	.01	ns
Occupation										
Lower	8.1	6.6	4.5	83	9.3	3.2	1.1	7.7	0.8	7.0
Middle	8.1	6.9	4.1	101	9.2	3.8	1.5	10.3	1.0	7.1
Upper	8.2	6.9	3.6	113	8.5	3.0	2.3	10.8	1.4	7.0
Probability	ns	ns	ns	.01	ns	.01	.01	.01	ns	ns
Income										
$0– 3,999	7.9	6.3	5.8	86	8.0	3.5	1.3	11.0	0.5	6.7
4,000– 9,999	8.1	6.9	4.3	93	9.6	3.6	1.2	8.7	1.3	7.1
10,000–14,999	8.3	6.6	3.0	106	9.1	3.3	1.9	9.3	1.2	7.0
15,000+	8.3	7.2	3.2	122	8.4	2.8	2.9	11.2	1.3	7.2
Probability	.01	.01	.01	.01	.01	.05	.01	.01	ns	ns
Class										
Working & lower	2.0	6.3	4.5	88	9.6	3.0	0.9	7.6	0.3	6.6
Middle	1.9	6.7	4.3	101	8.9	3.7	1.8	9.6	1.1	7.1
Upper & upper middle	1.6	7.3	3.3	112	8.2	3.1	2.5	12.7	2.1	7.4
Probability	.01	.01	.01	.01	.01	.01	.01	.01	.01	.01

See Appendix for description of variables.
Source. Second longitudinal study, round 1.

Table 2-11. *Relation of socioeconomic status to health, intelligence, social activity, and satisfaction.*

SES measure	Physical function	Health self-rating	Intelligence	Intimate contacts	Religious services	Meetings	Secondary contacts	Happiness	Total satisfaction
Education									
0- 6	4.1	3.5	54	6.4	2.8	2.4	3.7	4.0	33.1
7-12	3.9	3.6	77	6.7	2.6	2.3	4.0	4.2	34.8
13+	4.7	4.1	108	6.0	2.7	3.3	5.1	4.4	35.2
Probability	.01	.01	.01	ns	ns	.01	.01	ns	.05
Occupation									
Lower	4.0	3.5	52	6.4	2.7	2.3	3.5	3.8	32.7
Middle	4.1	3.6	73	6.6	2.8	2.5	4.1	4.4	34.5
Upper	4.7	4.0	107	6.0	2.7	3.2	5.2	4.3	35.3
Probability	.01	.01	.01	ns	ns	.01	.01	.01	.01
Finances									
Low	4.2	3.4	57	6.2	2.7	2.4	3.6	3.7	31.3
Middle	4.2	3.8	83	6.3	2.7	2.7	4.3	4.3	34.4
High	4.2	4.0	101	6.3	2.9	3.1	5.1	4.4	36.7
Probability	ns	.01	.01	ns	ns	.01	.01	.01	.01

* See Appendix A for description of variables.
Source. First longitudinal study, round 1.

associated with mental illness, this is an indication of greater mental health among the upper SES groups. Both studies also show a strong relationship between SES and intelligence scores, with mean scores of the upper groups being about 50 percent higher than the lower groups in the Adaptation Study, and twice as high in the old longitudinal study.

On the other hand, our studies show that the lower SES groups tend to have slightly *more* relatives and friends and *more* intimate contacts than upper SES groups. The differences are small and some of the relationships are not statistically significant, but the trend is consistent when SES is measured by education, occupation, or class. When SES is measured by income (second study) the highest and lowest income groups have less relatives and friends than the middle income groups. When SES is measured by the participants' estimates of their financial situation (first study) there are no significant differences in numbers of contacts with relatives and friends based on "intimate contacts" scores. Recall that previous studies have found little or no differences between SES and contacts with friends and relatives. Our findings indicate that this is true when SES is measured by income or finances, but that there are small but significant *negative* relationships when SES is measured by education or occupation.

There are little or no differences between SES groups in attendance at religious services, which agree with previous studies. However, in the second study there is a tendency for the middle SES groups to have slightly more attendance at religious services than the upper or lower groups.

The relationship between SES and attendance at nonreligious meetings is, nevertheless, strong and direct in both studies. In the second study the number of meetings attended by upper SES groups is several times greater than the number attended by lower SES groups. The differences are not as large in the first study, but are just as consistent and significant. The first study also shows that the number of secondary contacts (contacts with persons other than friends and relatives) are directly and consistently related to higher SES.

The second study shows that the number of hours spent in social activity is also directly and significantly related to higher SES, except for the lowest income group which reports almost as many social hours as the highest group. This is odd since the lowest income group has the least relatives and friends and attends meetings less. Perhaps they spend more time in religious services and concentrate their social activity on fewer friends and relatives.

Finally, happiness and total satisfaction are consistently and significantly related to higher SES in the first study. In the second study, the affect-balance score shows more positive affect reported by higher SES groups, although two of the relationships are not statistically significant. Life satisfaction is significantly higher among those identifying themselves as being in the upper or upper-middle classes, but is not significantly related to the other measures of SES.

In summary, our findings generally support the previous studies that show higher SES to be positively related to better physical and mental health, higher intelligence, more attendance at secular meetings, and greater happiness. However, there were little or no differences in contacts with friends and relatives, nor in attendance at religious services.

Table 2-12. *Significant effects of socioeconomic status on age changes.**

Age changes	Education increased R^2	p	Income increased R^2	p
Physician-rated health	.01	.05	.02	.05
Psychosomatic symptoms	.01	.05	.01	.05
Intelligence	.003	.01	.001	.05
Affect balance	.01	.05	.01	.05
Life satisfaction	.03	.01	.02	.01

* See Appendix for description of variables.
Source. Second longitudinal study.

Relation of SES to aging changes. Given this cross-sectional association between SES and various measures of health, activity, and happiness, the next question is whether there is a longitudinal association. Specifically, does higher SES contribute toward maintenance of better health, more activity and happiness as people age? There has been some theorizing that greater resources should help in adaptation to aging changes, but there has been no longitudinal analysis of SES effects on age changes.

We used a residual change analysis to test whether SES affected changes in health, activity, and satisfaction of the participants in our longitudinal studies. Specifically, among the second study participants who returned for the fourth examination, we used a series of regression analyses with the dependent variable being their score in the fourth examination on a series of measures of adaptation (health, activity, etc.); the first independent variable being their initial score on that measure (in order to control for initial levels); the second independent variable being their age at first examination (to control for age); and the third independent variable being either education or income. We then looked at the increases in variance explained (R^2) by adding that third variable.

Table 2-12 shows that five measures of adaptation showed significant (though small) effects of education and income on their changes in adaptation over the six-year period: physician's health rating, psychosomatic symptoms, intelligence, affect balance, and life satisfaction. This means that higher education and income helped maintain their adaptation in these areas compared to persons with lower education and income. Four other measures of adaptation were tested, but showed no significant effects: self-rated health, number of religious services attended, number of secular meetings attended, and number of social activity hours.

We also tried the same sort of analysis with the data from the first longitudinal study, but found only one significant effect, probably because there was only a small number of persons who survived and returned for the later rounds (for example, 110 in the fourth round).

To summarize, the second study shows that higher SES did tend to have small positive effects on maintaining health, cognitive function, and satisfaction over the six-year period of the study.

Summary

Elders tend to have lower socioeconomic status than younger persons. However, this is a mixture of cohort and aging effects. The lower education of elders is entirely due to cohort differences in that elders grew up in an era when there was less education in general. The lower occupations of elders is mainly a cohort effect, although some may have drifted down toward lower status occupations in old age. The lower income of elders is partly a cohort effect (due to their lower education and occupations) and partly an aging effect caused by retirement and/or disability. The longitudinal studies support these findings, but show less decline in adequacy of income than in amounts of income, and show no decline in feelings of status.

The factors determining income and assets of elders are similar to those for younger persons: primarily occupation, education, marital status, and number of children. Background factors having an independent effect are father's education and respondent's age. Data from the longitudinal studies show similar results to previous studies.

Previous studies have shown that higher socioeconomic status is related to better physical and mental health, better medical care, greater longevity, better cognitive function, more volunteer work, attendance at secular events, less social problems, and greater life satisfaction. SES does not seem to be related to church attendance or contacts with friends and relatives. The longitudinal studies tend to confirm these findings, but show that the lower SES groups tended to have slightly more relatives and friends and more intimate contacts. Futhermore, the second longitudinal study showed that higher SES tended to help maintain better health, better cognitive function, and higher satisfaction as the participants aged.

Chapter 3. Retirement

Retirement is clearly one of the most important social factors in aging. It affects the way elders spend their time, the amount of their income, their social interaction; and it may affect physical and mental health, self-esteem, and life satisfaction. It is also one of the most controversial factors in aging. On the individual level, there is the recurring question of whether to retire, and if so, when; and if retired, whether to do some part-time work or even return to full-time work. On the social level there is the current controversy over mandatory retirement with all the associated controversies over individual right to work *vs.* the organization's right to force retirement; the economic effects of mandatory retirement; the individual dangers *vs.* benefits of retirement; and the productivity of older workers. It is one of the most researched factors in aging and yet, as we shall see, there are substantial gaps remaining in our knowledge about retirement.

Two of the main issues are, why do people retire (voluntarily or involuntarily), and is retirement a crisis (does it produce poverty, illness, inactivity, and unhappiness?) We will examine longitudinal data relevant to both these issues.

Age, Period, and Cohort Effects

A preliminary problem is that of definition. There is no single agreed-upon definition of retirement. Rather there are numerous definitions in use and each is useful for certain purposes. The most strict definition, which includes the smallest number of people, defines retired persons as only those who have worked in the past but who had *no* work experience during the past year. This definition includes about two-thirds of men over age 65 and about four-fifths of women over 65 (Palmore, 1967). In order of greater inclusiveness are the following definitions: (1) not in the labor force during the survey week; (2) not usually at full-time job in peceding year; (3) not at work during the survey week; (4) receiving retirement benefits; (5) less than 6 months of full-time work in preceding year; and (6) less than full-time, year-round work. This last, most inclusive definition includes about 90 percent of men and 95 percent of women over age 65. One can also define retirement as a continuous variable, such as number of weeks not employed during the year (Palmore, 1971). This is a measure of "degree of retirement" ranging from zero for completely employed to 52 for completely retired. We shall use a variety of definitions depending on the available date.

National Data

It is clear that male retirement has been increasing in frequency while female retirement has been decreasing. What has not been previously analyzed is how much of these changes in retirement rate are due to age, period, or cohort effects. Table 3-1 shows the necessary data for an analysis of age, period, and cohort effects on retirement (percent not in labor force) among men and women in the U.S.A. from 1940 through 1978. Notice that the period intervals (10 years) equal the years

Table 3-1. *Percentage not in labor force by sex, age, period, and cohort (U.S.A.).*

Age	1940	1950	1960	1970	1980
Men					
50-59	10	11	10	11	13
60-69	30	29	38	42	53
70+	72	72	78	83	86
Women					
50-59	80	71	57	50	49
60-69	88	83	77	72	76
70+	96	95	93	93	95

Source. For 1940-1970: U.S. Census Bureau, *Employment status and work experience.* Washington: USGPO, 1973. For 1978: U.S. Bureau of Labor Statistics, *Employment and earnings,* April, 1978. Vol. 25, No. 4. Washington: 1978.

covered by each cohort so that the necessary three-way comparisons can be made. The last period, 1978, should be 1980, but 1980 data are not yet available and 1978 is used as an estimate of what 1980 data will be like.

This table shows that there are generally all three kinds of possible differences: cross-sectional (read down the columns), longitudinal (read across descending diagonals), and time-lag (read across the rows). When all three differences are observed, it is impossible to separate age, from cohort, from period effects with certainty (Palmore, 1978).

However, the most likely interpretation appears to be the following. There have been little or no cohort effects as shown by the facts that all cohorts of men in their 50s and of women in their 70s are similar in their retirement rates. In other words, there does not appear to have been any general differences between cohorts which would make all age groups retire more or less. But there is a strong age effect for both men and women at all periods and among all cohorts. However, this age effect has gradually increased over time among both men and women. Each succeeding male cohort starts out at about the same retirement rate during their 50s but increases its retirement rate in their 60s and 70s over that of the previous cohort. Each succeeding female cohort, on the other hand, starts out in their 50s with a lower retirement rate and ends up at the same retirement rate in their 70s.

The increasing age effect among men is probably due to the increasing retirement benefits that have become available in recent periods. The increasing age effect among women is probably due to their increasing labor force participation in recent periods. Thus, there appears to have been strong period effects which have increased the age effect on retirement of both men and women.

Data from the Longitudinal Studies

When the data from the longitudinal studies are plotted in composite figures, they show similar trends to the national data. Figure 3-1 shows the changes between pairs of rounds in percent not employed from the first longitudinal study, for all persons in each pair of round, except that women listing "housewife" as primary life-time occupation have been omitted. These lines show that even with housewives omitted, women generally retire more than men. The women's lines increase from 65 percent not employed in round 1 when their average was 70, to all not employed in round 5 when average age was about 80. (Employment was not coded after round 6.) The men's percentage increased from 53 to 76.

Figure 3-2 shows the changes in percent retired from full-time work for the 6-year age cohorts in the second longitudinal study over the 6-year interval of the study. This shows that while most men were working full-time around age 50, most were retired by their early 70s. Women started off with 40 percent retired and ended with all retired by their 70s. There was a higher percentage of women than men retired at each age.

Determinants of Retirement

In this section we will try to answer the general question, "Why do people retire?" There are two ways we can approach this complicated question: we can simply ask people why they retired or we can analyze which demographic and job characteristics are actually associated with retirement. The latter approach changes the question to, "Which types of people are likely to retire from which kinds of jobs?"

While there have been numerous studies of why people retire, there remains some controversy about the relative importance of various factors: the value of subjective reasons as opposed to objective characteristics; how to classify reasons as voluntary or involuntary; and how to estimate the main reason when there are several reasons involved.

Previous Studies

The most comprehensive and systematic study of why people retire was based on a national survey carried out by the Social Security Administration in 1963 (Palmore, 1971). When people were asked in this survey why they retired, about two-thirds gave involuntary reasons such as poor health, being "too old" to work, or being forced to retire by mandatory retirement policies. Of these reasons, poor health or being "too old" to work was the most frequent (43 percent of men, 36 percent of women). Less than a third of the retired men said they retired for voluntary reasons such as preferring leisure. Over half (58 percent) of the retired women gave voluntary reasons, but this is difficult to interpret because about 20 percent of the women gave both voluntary and involuntary reasons for retirement. It will be interesting to see if the new law against mandatory retirement until age 70 reduces the proportion of retirees who say they retire for involuntary reasons.

When the various demographic characteristics associated with retirement are analyzed, it is clear that age is by far the single most important variable. It alone doubles the amount of variance explained, even after all other demographic variables are taken into account. This means that the tendency for older workers to

Figure 3-1. *Percentage not employed by year and sex.*

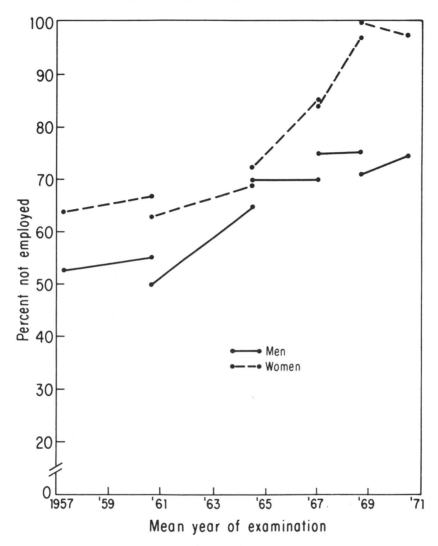

Note.—Men = 92 in rounds 1 and 2; women = 42 in rounds 1 and 2, omitting those limiting "housewife" as their primary occupation.
    Source. First longitudinal study. Employment data was not collected after round 6.

retire more cannot be explained away by the association of age with illness, lack of education, marital status, or other factors. This independent influence of age on retirement is probably due mainly to discrimination in employment, the general expectation that older persons should retire more, and the greater availability of more retirement benefits for older workers.

    Poor health was the second most important factor among men. This has the

Figure 3-2. *Percentage retired by age cohort and sex (rounds 1 to 4).*

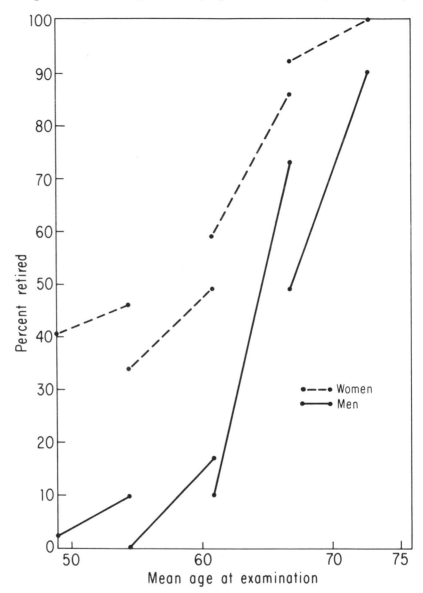

Note.—Retired is defined as less than full-time work.
Source. Second longitudinal study.

obvious interpretation that ill and disabled men retire more, but there is the possibility that some of this relationship may be due to a justification of retirement in terms of poor health.

The second most important demographic factor for the total aged is sex.

Regardless of how it is measured, women retire much more (or keep working less) than men. For example, only about half as many women as men over 65 continue to work, either full or part time (Harris, 1975). Also, women over 62 work only about one-third as many weeks in the year as men, on average (Palmore, 1971). Of course some women (about 5 percent) never held regular full-time jobs and so have not "retired" in the usual sense. However, if we eliminated these women from the analysis, it would change the results very little. This greater retirement rate among women, as well as the higher proportion of women who retire for voluntary reasons, can be explained by a simple principle derived from role theory. In the present generation of older persons, the worker role is more important to men than to women. This is probably due to different socialization processes between boys and girls, different expectations of others including spouses, and employment discrimination between the sexes. However, with greater equality between the sexes, retirement rates of men and women are converging.

The second most important factor among women was marital status: married women retired much more than never married women and somewhat more than ex-married women. This is related to the sources of retirement support from the husband of the married women, on the one hand, and to the greater work experience as well as greater need for earnings among the never married women. Among men, marital status had the opposite effect: married men retire less, probably because they tend to be younger, healthier, and have greater need for earnings.

The next most important demographic factor was education: more highly educated persons tended to retire later and less often. There are probably several explanations for the influence. First, the better educated are more likely to be doing types of work not so affected by the declining physical abilities of advancing years. Second, the work of the better educated tends to be more interesting and rewarding. Third, the educated probably face less employment discrimination because their skills are in greater demand, and they are more likely to be self-employed, hence less likely to face compulsory retirement.

The above description of reasons for retirement applies primarily to persons retiring after the usual retirement age of 65. Persons retiring before age 65 seem to fall into two main types: those retiring because of disability and those voluntarily retiring because of an attractive pension plan (Barfield & Morgan, 1969). There is much less mandatory retirement among early retirees (Reno, 1971).

The relative influence of retirement income on the retirement decision is rather uncertain. It does seem to be most important among healthy early retirees (Barfield & Morgan, 1969), and is especially important among semiskilled workers (Simpson & McKinney, 1966). Most skilled and white collar workers apparently feel their retirement income will be sufficient, and there is little relation between income and retirement among these workers (Streib & Schneider, 1971).

The third type of analysis related to why people retire has to do with the type of job. In general blue-collar (manual) workers retire more than white-collar workers. This is in turn related to the three reasons discussed under education: blue-collar jobs are more physically demanding, less rewarding, and have more mandatory

Table 3-2. *Reasons for retirement.*

Reason	Men	Women
Poor health or disability	16%	22%
Compulsory retirement, laid off, etc.	40	35
Total involuntary	56	57
Financial (eligible for pension, could afford to retire)	10	2
Recreational (wanted to enjoy leisure)	15	13
Family (wanted to spend more time with family, needed at home)	1	20
Other voluntary	18	8
Total voluntary	44	43
Grand total	100	100

Note.—Men = 93; women = 60.
Source. Duke second longitudinal study, round 4.

retirement. When jobs were rated in terms of job strain, the heavier jobs were related to more willingness to retire (Jacobson, 1972). Similarly, those in less autonomous jobs were more willing to retire. Also "low quality jobs" (those with less autonomy, variety, and responsibility) are related to more willingness to retire (Sheppard, 1972). Finally, lower skilled auto workers were much more likely to retire early than higher skilled auto workers (Sheppard, 1976).

The Duke Longitudinal Studies

The second study asked its retirees, "Why did you retire?" as did the Social Security Administration (SSA) survey. However, there were two main differences in the way the responses were coded (Table 3-2). First, if more than one reason was given, we asked for the main reason and coded only one reason. Second, we limited the "poor health" category to illness or disability, and did not include the vague "too old" response in this category, as did the SSA. This had the result of reducing the most frequent reason given in the SSA survey ("poor health or too old") from 43 percent for men and 36 percent for women to 16 percent for men and 22 percent for women in our study ("poor health" only). On the other hand, the proportion giving compulsory retirement or some other involuntary reason increased to 40 percent for men and 35 percent for women. As a result the totals giving involuntary reasons were similar in the two studies: a little over 60 percent in the SSA survey; a little under 60 percent in our study. Thus, both studies agree that a majority of retirees retire for involuntary reasons, even though there were substantial differences in the frequency of specific involuntary reasons.

Another similarity between the two studies is the fact that while almost no men gave "family" reasons ("needed at home" in the SSA survey), substantial proportions of women gave this as their main reason for retiring (20 percent in the second longitudinal study). This again illustrates the fact that many women workers in the age group consider their family role more important than their work role, while few men do so.

While looking at attitudes toward retirement, we noticed a peculiar thing. About 80 percent of persons aged 46-64 were working and said they would continue to work even if they "did not actually have to work for a living." Presumably this meant that most found their work so satisfying that they wanted to continue working even if they did not need the money and could retire. Yet, beyond the age of 65 less than a third actually did continue to work. One explanation for the shift would be that compulsory retirement or poor health forces them to retire. Another would be that because of social norms in favor of retirement, these workers changed their attitude toward work when they reached the "normal" retirement age of 65, and voluntarily retired.

In order to find out the relative importance of these alternate explanations, we looked at the reasons for retirement after age 65 given by those under age 65 at the beginning of the study, who had said they wanted to continue working even though they did not actually have to work for a living ($N = 35$). It turned out that about two-thirds said they had to retire because of poor health or compulsory retirement, but the other third apparently changed their minds after age 65 and decided that they wanted to retire for voluntary reasons.

Turning now to the characteristics of those who retired, we did multivariable regression analysis with retired status as the dependent (dummy) variable, and age, occupation (manual vs. nonmanual), marital status (married vs. nonmarried), education, and physical function rating as the independent variables. Only age and physical function were significantly related to retirement. Age was a stronger factor among women, but among men age was of equal importance as physical function. Together, age and physical function accounted for 25 percent of the variance in retirement. The effects of age could not be explained by the other factors, because when age was entered the equation after all the other factors, it more than doubled the variance explained. This confirms the finding of the earlier Social Security Administration Study that there is something about aging itself (age discrimination, pension eligibility, changes in role expectations, pressures from friends and fellow workers) which markedly increases retirement, and which is independent of physical abilities or demographic characteristics.

Consequences of Retirement

An understanding of the consequences of retirement is essential for intelligent personal decision as to whether or not to retire, and for optimum retirement policies. There are widespread myths about the effects of retirement: some which exaggerate dire consequences such as loneliness, poverty, illness, and death; and some which point to retirement as the problem-free "golden years."

Previous Studies

Income. One of the most common fears about retirement is the fear of poverty or at least severe loss of income. Such fears are generally unwarranted. We pointed out in the previous chapter that only 14 pecent of persons over 65 have incomes below the federal poverty levels. Since 12 percent of persons under 65 are also in poverty, most of the persons over 65 in poverty have probably been in poverty, or near poverty, before age 65. Therefore, if a person has avoided poverty before retirement, the chances are excellent that he/she will avoid it after retirement.

On the other hand, income can be expected to decline substantially because of retirement. Previous studies have found average declines of around one-half, although this decline may be less in recent years because of improving social security and pension income. However, there are many offsetting factors which usually reduce the impact of income decline, such as reduced expenses, accumu-lated assets, tax benefits, free or discounted goods and services, and a guaranteed minimum income (SSI). Furthermore, the fear that inflation will erode retirement income is probably no more warranted than at other ages, because social security benefits and many other pensions are now protected against inflation by automatic cost-of-living increases.

Therefore, the *adequacy* of most people's income declines less than the *actual* income decline (Streib & Schneider, 1971). In other words, while most retirees have less income than before retirement, most still find their income to be about as adequate as before retirement.

Illness and mortality. Another widespread fear is that retirement will cause illness and an early death. This fear is also generally unwarranted. There is no good evidence to support it. It is true that many people retire *because* of failing health and die soon after. This is why retired persons as a group have more illness and higher mortality rates than nonretired. But all the controlled studies agree that failing health is the *cause* of retirement, not the *consequence* of retirement.

For example, a study of persons retired under compulsory retirement policies (which included healthy as well as unhealthy persons) found that their mortality rate was no different from all persons their age (Myers, 1954). Similarly, a previous longitudinal study of retirement found that health declined with age, but not with retirement (Streib & Schneider, 1971). In other words, retired people were no more likely to be sick than people their same age who were still on the job. In fact, unskilled workers showed a slight *improvement* in average health following retire-ment.

Undoubtedly, some people suffer from retirement, experience declining health, and die earlier than if they had kept working. These are likely to be people whose life was wrapped up in their work and are unable or unwilling to find satisfactory work-substitutes in retirement. Or they may be people who "retire to the rocking chair," become completely inactive or isolated. Or retirement may have caused such a severe drop in income that they cannot afford the necessities to keep them healthy. Studies do find a minority of retirees who report poorer health after retirement.

However, this minority is more or less balanced by those whose health and longevity improves upon retirement. These are likely to be people whose jobs were bad for their health, or who disliked their work, or they may have increased various activities which contribute to better health and longevity. Thus, the balance between those with declining health and those with improving health leaves the average health of retirees unchanged, except for the usual effects of aging.

Mental illness. Much the same can be said for the effects of retirement on mental illness. It is true that most mentally ill aged are among the "retired," because most aged who become mentally ill must quit work. Here again the mental illness is the cause of retirement rather than vice versa. There have been numerous studies of the effects of retirement on mental disorders and some of them have found definite evidence that retirement can cause mental illness (Nadelson, 1969).

As was the case with physical illness, some retired do become mentally ill, but their illness is most likely the result of poor health, low social activity, or unsatisfactory living arrangements rather than of retirement itself (Lowenthal & Berkman, 1967). Under conditions of relatively high socioeconomic status, retirement, itself, seems to make little or no psychiatric difference. Again, those few whose mental health is impaired by retirement are apparently balanced by those whose mental health is improved by release from a stressful job.

Life satisfaction. Another common fear is that retirement will cause unhappiness or depression. All the studies agree that this is generally not true. For example, the Cornell Study of Occupational Retirement found that average life satisfaction scores did not show a pattern of decline after retirement; that about 80 percent of retirees said that stopping work did *not* make them feel less satisfied and only 10 percent said it did; about 80 percent said that retirement is mostly good for a person and this percentage increased the longer the person had been retired (Streib & Schneider, 1971). Similarly, a study of retired teachers and telephone company employees found that 83 percent liked retirement and that no group in their study had as much as 10 percent with a high degree of depression (Cottrell & Atchley, 1969). Finally, an earlier Duke study found that morale was generally unconnected to work or retirement (Simpson & McKinney, 1966).

Again, it should be recognized that retirement does make a small minority unhappy. These tend to be people who were forced into retirement, or who could not find satisfactory substitutes for the work role, or who suffered severe loss of income. Also because there is often some choice in the matter, those who would be unhappy in retirement often manage to keep working. About two-thirds of those who keep working think retirement would be mostly a bad thing (Streib & Schneider, 1971).

Social activity. The final myth about retirement is that it generally causes inactivity, isolation, and loneliness. Again the studies agree that it may for a few, but not for most retirees. About half the retired teachers and telephone employees reported that retirement has made no change in the number of contacts with friends, about 30 percent reported an *increase* in contacts, and only 20 percent reported a decrease (Cottrell & Atchley, 1969). Similarly, three-fourths reported the same or more participation in organizations following retirement. In addition, three-fourths felt lonely "hardly ever" or "not at all." Also widowhood accounted for a large proportion of those lonely.

The earlier Duke study found that about half of the retirees reported *some* decline in social activity, such as dropping out of an organization, reducing the number of friends, or losing some interest (Simpson & McKinney, 1966). However, the average amount of decline was only one point on a seven-point scale: the equivalent of dropping out of one organization or one interest. It is also noteworthy that about half reported *no* decline in social activity.

The Duke Longitudinal Studies*

The effects of retirement. Three methods were used to determine the effects of retirement: (1) direct questioning, (2) a repeated measures analysis of variance, and (3) a residual change analysis. Each method has some advantages over the others but they generally yield consistent results. The direct questioning method consisted of asking retired persons to estimate how much effect retirement had on their income, satisfaction, etc. The repeated measures analysis of variance used all the scores on a given effect available on those who retired during the second longitudinal study and compared the scores before retirement with those after retirement. The residual change method (as described earlier) used the initial score as a control variable and then looked for changes after retirement that are significantly different from the expected change (Palmore et al., 1979).

1. Health. The repeated measures analysis found no significant changes after retirement in self-rated health, physician-rated health, weeks sick in bed, psychosomatic symptoms, or in eight other measures of illness. It did, however, find a slight decrease in the musculoskeletal system rating, and a substantial increase in the number of medications taken and in the number of symptoms checked after retirement (Palmore et al., 1979). Thus, there is relatively little evidence of substantial decline in health after retirement, and it seems likely that retirement because of declining health would account for the few changes that were observed.

2. Activity. The repeated measures analysis found many substantial changes in activity (Table 3-3). As would be expected, the number of hours worked declined by about 35. This was partly compensated for by increases in the hours of active leisure (+7), and of sedentary leisure (+10), but the largest increase was in hours of solitary leisure (+35). Similarly, the respondents' rating of how many people they interact with decreased (−1.1), and their rating of how busy they were decreased (−0.6). On the other hand, there were no decreases in attendance at religious services or other meetings. Also there was no significant change in number of friends and a slight *increase* (+.8) in number of neighbors known well enough to visit. These results were similar when the residual change method was used. Thus, there did appear to be a substantial drop in the total amount of active, productive, and social hours after retirement, because the decline in hours worked is only partially

---

*Clark Luikart, Ph.D., assisted in the analysis of data in this section. Data are from the second longitudinal study because most persons in the first study were already retired before the beginning of the study.

Table 3-3. *Significant * changes after retirement.*

Variable	Pre-retirement	Post-retirement	Change
Activity			
Hours worked (including travel)	48	13	−35
Hours of active leisure	25	32	+ 7
Hours of sedentary leisure	31	41	+10
Hours of solitary leisure	3	38	+35
Persons seen	5.7	4.6	− 1.1
Inactive–busy	5.6	5.0	− 0.6
Number neighbors	6.0	6.8	+ 0.8
Adaptation			
Income	$12,900	$9,348**	−$3,552
Percent too much free time	4	19	+15
Percent too little free time	35	9	−26

Note.— N = 75 individuals; 293 observations. Hours do not add to total hours in a week because sleep hours were not counted and some categories are not mutually exclusive.
    * Probability of change occuring by chance less than .01.
    ** In constant dollars.
    Source. Second longitudinal study.

compensated for by increases in active, productive, and social leisure. In this limited sense disengagement theory was supported: disengagement from work resulted in a net reduction of active, productive, and social pursuits.

3. Adaptation. The repeated measures method found a 28 percent decline in mean income (constant dollars) after retirement. This was less than reported in some other longitudinal studies. It is possible that our retirees are somewhat above average in this regard (as in other respects).

The direct questioning showed more retirees reporting a substantial decline in *actual* income (55 percent declined by one-fourth or more; 35 percent declined by one-half or more) than retirees reporting a decline in *adequacy* of income (9 percent).

There was a significant increase in the proportion who reported they had too much free time (+15 percent) and a corresponding decline in the proportion reporting that they had too little free time (−26 percent)—although it is interesting that even in retirement about a tenth still say they have too little free time.

The repeated measures analysis did not find significant changes in any of the measures of life satisfaction. However, the residual change analysis found small but significant decreases in life satisfaction, affect balance, and feelings of usefulness. Since the average decrease on these measures was less than one-half a standard deviation, it appears that most negative effects of retirement were either temporary or relatively minor. Table 3-4 shows that only 13 percent had substantial declines in life satisfaction after retirement and 20 percent had substantial declines in affect

Table 3-4. *Change in life satisfaction and affect balance after retirement.*

Change	Life satisfaction*	Affect balance**
Increase of more than 1 *SD*	11%	32%
Less than ± 1 *SD* change	76	48
Decrease of more than 1 *SD*	13	20
Total	100	100

Note.— N = 76.
* One standard deviation for life satisfaction (round 1) = 1.5
** One standard deviation for affect balance (round 1) = 2.7
Source. Second longitudinal study.

balance. These few who suffered substantial negative effects tended to be balanced by those who experienced positive effects. Another analysis found that being retired (not employed) had a small net *positive* effect on affect balance once other social status variables were controlled (George, 1978).

Effects of mandatory retirement and return to work. A special analysis was made of the effects of mandatory retirement and of return to part-time or full-time work in the first longitudinal study (Lowry, 1979). This analysis found that those who had retired for mandatory reasons were usually lower in activity levels and adjustment ratings compared to others. They were also lower in life satisfaction just following retirement, but apparently felt more satisfied in later stages.

Those retirees who returned to full-time work were higher than others in all three dimensions: activity, adjustment, and life satisfaction; and this was true in most stages of retirement. Life satisfaction fell sharply just after retirement, but improved rapidly as they became reemployed. Those retirees who returned to part-time work showed somewhat mixed trends with improvements in activity level and life satisfaction after settling into retirement, but with declines in their adjustment ratings. The implication of these findings appears to be that mandatory retirement tends to have negative effects, while return to work tends to have positive effects.

Predictors of life satisfaction after retirement. In order to explore what kinds of retirees are likely to be more satisfied after retirement, we did a residual change analysis of life satisfaction in the second longitudinal study. This analysis used life satisfaction after retirement as the dependent variable, the initial life satisfaction score as a control variable, and a series of possible predictors as the independent variables. The possible predictors were drawn from those variables previously found to be associated with life satisfaction in our study (Palmore & Luikart, 1974). Only three of these variables were significant predictors of life satisfaction after retirement (Table 3-5). The first and strongest predictor was the initial life satisfaction score, which alone explained 38 percent of the variance. This means that the best single predictor of satisfaction after retirement was the satisfaction before retirement. The second predictor was having a child still in the home. Apparently

Table 3-5. *Multiple regression of significant predictors* of life satisfaction after retirement.*

Variable	Zero=order correlation (r)	Variance (R²)	Unstandardized slope (b)
Preretirement life satisfaction	.62	.38	.71
Child in home	.14	.42	1.03
Self-identification as middle-aged	.22	.46	.59

Note.— N = 76.
* Increase in variance accounted for by each predictor was significant at .05 level.
Source. Second longitudinal study.

the child at home somehow aided the transition, perhaps by helping counter the loneliness that sometimes occurs.

The third predictor was self-identification as middle-aged. Apparently those who thought of themselves as younger (or "middle-aged" rather than "old" or "elderly") adjusted better and were more satisfied with retirement. This relationship held even when chronological age was controlled.

Summary

Retirement is one of the most important factors in aging; profoundly affecting income, activity, and interaction; subtly affecting health and satisfaction. Age effects on retirement have been increasing because of greater retirement benefit among men and greater labor force participation among women. About 90 percent of all workers have retired by age 70.

About two-thirds retire for involuntary reasons such as poor health or compulsory retirement policies. However, the frequencies of specific reasons differed in our adaptation study from others because of coding diferences: "poor health" was less frequent in the adaptation study. Age is the strongest single predictor of retirement, and only a small portion of its influence can be explained by its association with illness, lower education, marital status, or other demographic factors. The independent influence of age on retirement is probably due to age discrimination in employment, general expectations that older workers should retire, and retirement benefits for older workers. Women retire more than men, and manual workers retire more than nonmanual. The longitudinal studies were consistent with previous surveys in these findings.

Retirement does not usually cause a decrease in life satisfaction, and those few who are less satisfied after retirement tend to be balanced by those who are more satisfied after retirement. The Duke Studies did find small average decreases in life satisfaction and happiness, but most retirees had little or no such decreases. Indeed, retirement appears to have a small *positive* effect on happiness once other social variables are taken into account.

The Duke Studies found declines in productive, active, and social activities after retirement, but no decline in number of religious services or other meetings attended. Few retirees became completely inactive, isolated, or very lonely. However, mandatory retirement tended to have negative effects on life satisfaction, adjustment, and activity; while return to work tended to have positive effects.

The best predictors of life satisfaction after retirement were life satisfaction before retirement, having a child in the home, and self-identification as "middle-aged" (rather than "old" or "elderly").

Thus to answer the two questions with which we began this chapter: the majority of workers retire because they have to, and yet very few suffer poverty, illness, inactivity, or depression as a result. Most appear to adapt to the "crisis" of retirement with little or no lasting negative effects.

Chapter 4. Social Activity

This chapter deals with some of the most controversial questions in social gerontology. Do elders reduce their social activity? Do most elders continue to maintain the same levels of activity relative to their age peers? Do elders become more alike or different in their social activities? Does social activity maintain or reduce life satisfaction and longevity?

By social activity, we mean any activity which involves interaction with other persons. However, this chapter will focus on nonwork social activity since previous chapters have dealt with work and retirement. This chapter will emphasize the quantity of social activity, while the following chapter on social networks will emphasize the types of persons involved in interaction with elders.

Aging Effects

Previous Research

Total social activity. Disengagement theory was the first assertion that social activity tends to decline among most elders (Cumming & Henry, 1961). In their cross-sectional study of 200 healthy middle-class residents of Kansas City over age 50, Cumming and Henry found that few of those over age 75 reported high social activity (between 8 and 27 percent depending on the measure) compared to those aged 50-54 (between 61 and 86 percent).

Similarly, a study of 500 elders over age 60 in New York City found that only 30 percent of those over age 75 had a "broad range of interpersonal relations" compared to 52 percent of those aged 60-64 (Kutner, 1956). A study of 250 elders over age 60 in Kentucky also found that nearly half reported decreases in social activity since age 50, but only 3 percent reported increases (Youmans, 1962).

More recently, a study of 1,441 adult residents of Houston, Texas, found that there was a high negative association between age and social activities, while there was no association between age and solitary activities (Gordon & Gaitz 1976). However, some types of activities were exceptions to this general pattern: club activity, entertaining, and discussions were not lower among elders.

Therefore, while most of the studies tend to agree that total social activity tends to decline with age, there are several reservations to keep in mind. First, some types of social activity appear not to decline with age. These are discussed in the following sections. Second, since none of these studies were longitudinal, we do not know how much of the differences between age groups is due to aging and how much is due to cohort differences. Furthermore, even though the average may have declined, we do not know how many may have maintained or even increased their level of social activity. We turn now to a discussion of various types of social activity which usually do not fit the general pattern of decline.

Informal social activity. This includes interaction with family, friends, and neighbors. The most recent national evidence on changes in informal social activity comes form the Harris survey (1975). This survey constructed a "Social and Family Contact Scale" based on the frequency of contacts with friends and relatives and found that there were almost identical median scores for those under and over age 65, although there was a small drop among those over age 80. However, there were less of those 65+ compared to those 18-74 who reported spending "a lot of time" socializing with friends (8 percent less), caring for younger or older members of the family (26 percent less), and participating in sports (19 percent less). Other studies have found a decline with age in such informal social activities as dancing and drinking, going to movies and sports events, and travel (Gordon & Gaitz, 1976).

Voluntary associations. Cross-sectional studies have consistently found a curvilinear pattern of age and participation in voluntary associations: participation is low in the 20s, rising to a peak around age 40, and then declining after age 45 (Cutler, 1977). However, when socioeconomic status is controlled, the pattern is generally one of stable or increasing levels of membership and participation after age 45 through at least ages 75-80. Only after age 80 does infirmity and limitations on mobility begin to lower participation appreciably (Cutler 1976a; Nie et al., 1974; Harris, 1975; Babchuk et al., 1979). Longitudinal and retrospective studies agree that voluntary association participation tends to be stable in late life (Videbeck & Knox, 1965; Babchuk & Booth, 1969; Bell, 1971; Cutler, 1977) or increases somewhat (Atchley, 1976; Johnson, 1975). Thus, previous research on voluntary association participation does not usually fit the disengagement pattern.

Religious activity. There is a widespread assumption that religious activity tends to increase with age. This is one of the most frequent misconceptions that appear in surveys of knowledge about aging (Palmore, 1977). However, cross-sectional studies and two limited previous longitudinal studies agree that church attendance is generally at a high level in the 60s, but becomes less regular with advancing old age (Riley & Foner, 1968; Harris, 1975). On the other hand, private religious practices such as Bible reading and prayer are generally reported in greater percentages of elderly than the young (Fukuyama, 1961; Erskine, 1965; Cavan et al., 1949). But these are all cross-sectional studies and so the greater percentages of elderly reporting private religious practices may simply be cohort differences rather than age effects.

Political participation. The aged are less involved in the more active forms of political participation such as canvassing neighborhoods and activity working for a candidate, but this appears to be due to infirmity, larger proportions female, and lower education levels rather than to falling political interest (Hudson & Binstock, 1976; Harris, 1975). There is a roughly linear positive relation between age and political interest, and when controls for sex and education are introduced, the increase with age becomes even greater. Also when sex and socioeconomic status are controlled, those over 65 have the highest voting rate of any age group (Verba & Nie, 1972; Glenn & Grimes, 1968). Thus, previous studies indicate that it is only the most active (and infrequent) forms of political participation that decline with age.

Homogeneity vs. *heterogeneity.* It is clear that differentiation increases during early life. The question is whether differentiation continues throughout the middle and later year. Many developmentalists have argued that heterogeneity in life style and functioning increases during later life (Bromley, 1966; Havighurst, 1957; Riegel, 1971; Riegel et al., 1967; Neugarten, 1964). On the other hand, several theorists have argued that as activity declines and the common denominator of death is approached, the aged become increasingly alike (Kelly, 1955; Riegel et al., 1967). A related controversy is whether the two sexes tend to become more alike in old age as the men retire, women lose their child-rearing functions, and both reduce sexual activity (Cameron, 1968); or whether the "sexes become increasingly divergent with age" (Neugarten, 1964). These controversies have continued largely because there has not been adequate longitudinal data available to resolve the issues. A previously published analysis of the first Duke longitudinal study found that when mortality and other losses were controlled, the variability of a number of social, psychological, and physiological measures tended to be maintained or increased (Maddox & Douglas, 1974). Specifically, variability in the total social activity score showed no consistent trend over the first six rounds of examination.

Continuity. The question here is whether individuals tend to maintain the same rank order on a given activity as they age or tend to change rank order as some increase and others decrease. One might speculate that with all the profound life events of aging such as retirement, widowhood, changed living arrangements, and illness, there would be little continuity in life styles or social activity over the years. On the other hand, there is the general belief that aged people get "set in there ways" and do not change much. There has been no definitive research on this question, again largely because of the absence of relevant longitudinal data. One retrospective study found that nine-tenths of both the high and low (quartile) social participants would have had similar scores five years earlier (Videbeck & Knox, 1965). A previous report on the first Duke longitudinal study also reported a moderately high persistence of rank order on total social activity scores from the first to the sixth round of examinations (Spearman Rho = .55; Maddox & Douglas, 1974).

B. The Duke Longitudinal Studies

Total social activities. Both the first and second longitudinal studies show slow but steady declines in the means of total social activities as the participants age. In the first longitudinal study, the mean sum of intimate contacts and leisure activities scores (which include the number of leisure social activites, number of organizations belonged to, and number of meetings attended) drops for both men and women by about 3 points from the first round of examinations to the eleventh examination (Figure 4-1). This figure shows mean scores on each pair of rounds for the men and women present at each pair of rounds (e.g. rounds 1 and 2, rounds 2 and 3, etc.)

The patterns are similar for both men and women, and for older (70+ at round 1) and younger (60-69 at round 1) participants, but the younger participants decline somewhat less than the older participants. In the total group the correlation (Pearson r) between year of examination and this social activity score was $-.40$, which indicates a moderately strong association.

Figure 4-1. *Total intimate contacts and leisure activities scores for pairs of rounds by year and sex.*

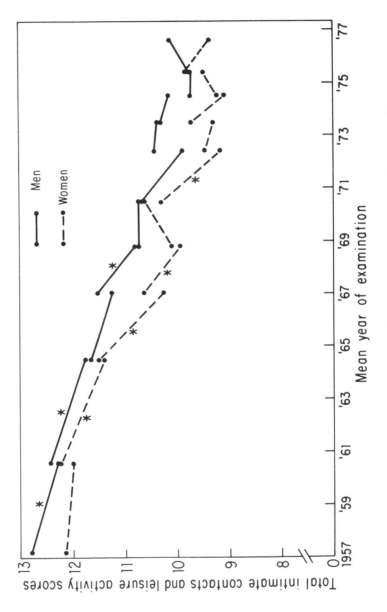

Note.— In rounds 1 and 2, men = 89, women = 87. In rounds 10 and 11, men = 12, women = 25.
* Change was significant at .05 level.
Source. First longitudinal study.

Figure 4-2. *Number of social hours by age cohort and sex (rounds 1 to 4).*

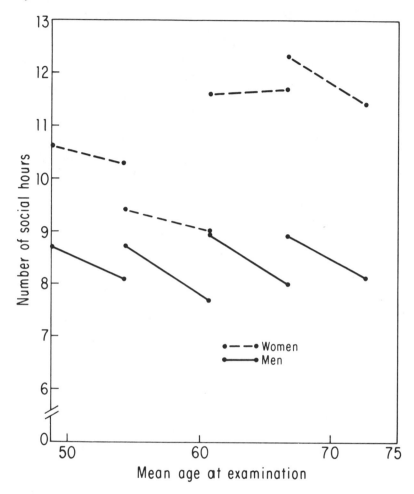

Source. Second longitudinal study.

In the second longitudinal study, the mean sum of social leisure hours (which include going to sports events, meetings, volunteer work, visiting, and entertaining) drops in most cohorts of men and women (Figure 4-2). This decline is similar for men and women, except that women have more social hours and one cohort shows no significant change.

As one might expect, just as social hours decrease, the mean number of solitary hours per week increases steadily in each cohort for a total increase of 15 hours, and the increase is greater for men than for women. For men, the greatest increase is during the normal retirement period, between the ages of 58 to 63 and 64 to 70. There is also a cumulative increase (over the 24-year period) of 17 percentage points in the number who say they spent most of their leisure time alone.

However, these steady declines in total social activity represent only the average of the entire group. There is considerable variation in social activity within the group at any one point in time and in the amount and direction of change over time. The standard deviations for the sum of intimate contacts and leisure activities in the first longitudinal study were around three points; and the standard deviations for the social activity hours in the second longitudinal study were around six hours. Many of the participants reported no declines and some reported increases in social activity. For example, in the first longitudinal study between rounds 1 and 3 (an eight-year interval), 20 percent had less than a one-point change in either direction and six percent had increases of one point or more. Similarly, in the second longitudinal study between rounds 1 and 4 (a six-year interval), 17 percent reported less than a one-hour change in either direction and 32 percent reported increases of one or more hours. Only half reported declines of one or more hours.

In summary, the evidence from both longitudinal studies show over-all patterns of gradual disengagement from total social activity for both men and women, old and young, but this pattern is not universal and there are substantial minorities who maintain or even increase their social activity as they age.

Informal social activity. Evidence from both longitudinal studies also indicates a gradual average decrease in the informal social activities of interaction with family and friends. In the first longitudinal study the "intimate contacts" scores tended to decline the same way total social activities declines. Eight of the ten intervals had decline in intimate contacts. Similarly, the rating of "primary group activities" tended to decline except in the eleventh round.

In the second longitudinal study, the weekly hours categories of visting, telephoning, or writing friends or relatives, parties, eating out, or entertaining showed small but consistent declines in each cohort over the six-year interval. If these declines are summed for the four cohorts covering 24 years, they add up to two hours (per week) decline over the 24-year interval.

Formal social activity. In the first longitudinal study, the mean rating of "secondary group contacts" tended to remain around the initial level throughout the twenty years of examinations. However, the participants were asked to compare their present attendance at clubs and churches with their attendance when they were age 55. Two-thirds of the men, but only two-fifths of the women said they were attending clubs less now than at age 55 (Table 4-1). Similarly, few men, but almost two-fifths of the women said they were attending more than at age 55. Thus, it appears that club activity declined more among men than women. Perhaps this was linked to the greater importance of retirement for men and an associated decline in participation in work-related clubs. Also, those over age 70 at the beginning of the study had somewhat higher proportions reporting that they attended less now than at age 55 (59 percent for 70+; 50 percent for 60–69). This indicates more frequent decline at older ages.

Men and women were similar to each other on church attendance with almost half reporting declines compared to less than a fifth reporting increases (Table 4-1). Also a somewhat larger proportion of older participants reported declines com-

Table 4-1. *Comparison of present club and church attendance to age 55 attendance.*

	Clubs			Churches		
	Men	Women	Total	Men	Women	Total
More now	13%	37%	25%	14%	20%	17%
Same	17	22	20	41	36	38
Less now	69	42	55	45	44	45
Total	100	100	100	100	100	100

Note.— N = 265
Source. First longitudinal study, round 1.

pared to the younger participants (46 percent *vs.* 42 percent). Similarly, change in the religious activities scale tends to show an irregular pattern until it begins to decline after the fourth round of examinations when the average age was about 80.

In the second longitudinal study there were no substantial changes in hours spent in meetings, except in the oldest cohort (age 64-70) which had a decline of one half-hour per week. The number of club meetings attended also remained fairly stable for both men and women (Figure 4-3). However, the number of church meetings attended usually showed an *increase* after the mid-50s among both men and women (Figure 4-3). Comparison of the evidence from the two studies indicates that church attendance tended to increase in late middle age and then decrease in late old age.

In terms of political participation, the only evidence we have comes from the second longitudinal study which found little or no change in proportions registered to vote.

Heterogeneity. There is no clear evidence from either study that people become more alike or different as they age. The standard deviations (a measure of how similar or different people are) show no consistent trends over time on any of the social activity variables. Apparently older persons tend to maintain, but not increase, their individual differences as they age. Furthermore, there were no consistent trends in differences between men and women as they age. On some variables, such as church attendance and informal social activity, there is a slight increase in differences between men and women, but there were no trends toward greater similarity, as has been suggested in the literature.

Continuity. Both longitudinal studies show evidence of strong continuity in social activity variables. For example, the sum of intimate contacts and leisure activities has a correlation (Peasonian *r*) of .65 between the round 1 and round 2 scores. This means that about half of the variance in the round 2 scores are explained by the scores in round 1, which occurred about four years earlier. This correlation tends to decline as the interval between rounds increases, but the correlation between the first and eleventh rounds was still .24. In the second longitudinal study, correlations between early and later scores ranged from .40 for round 1 with round 4 number of social hours, to .72 for round 1 with round 2 number of church meetings. However a special analysis of how many individuals

Figure 4-3. *Number of church and club meetings attended by age cohort and sex (rounds 1 to 4).*

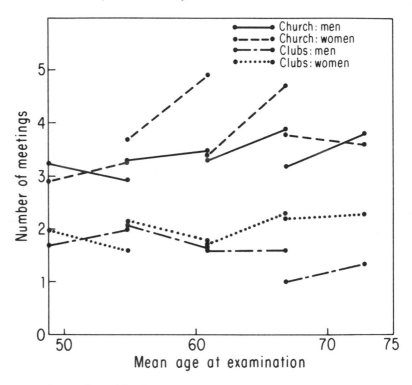

Source. Second longitudinal study.

stayed in the same quartile of social activities found that half changed quartiles in at least one round for church attendance, 56 percent changed quartiles for club attendance, 72 percent changed quartiles in hours spent on hobbies, 77 percent changed quartiles in hours in meetings, 84 percent changed quartiles in hours watching TV, and 85 percent changed quartiles in hours in social activities and in numbers of persons interacted with daily (Fox, 1979). Thus, while there was considerable continuity between any two rounds, most individuals showed some fluctuation in at least one round during the study.

Factors Affecting Social Activity

Previous Research

The limited research on determinants of social activity is consistent in regard to the influence of health, marital status, and living arrangements, but contradictory in regard to socioeconomic status and sex. All the studies agree that being healthy contributes to more social activity, whether among Spanish-American War veterans (Scotch & Richardson, 1966), or among the San Francisco elders (Lowenthal

& Berkman, 1967), or New York elders (Kutner, 1956), or Durham, North Carolina elders (Center for the Study of Aging & Human Development, 1978).

Similarly, all the studies agree that being currently married contributes to more social activity (Scotch & Richardson, 1966; Lowenthal & Berkman, 1967; Center for the Study of Aging and Human Development, 1978; Tallmer & Kutner, 1970); just as living with others does also (Kutner, 1956; Tallmer & Kutner, 1970).

The relationship between socioeconomic status (SES) and social activity appears more ambiguous and complex. The majority of studies have found those with higher SES to be more active socially (Kutner, 1956; Lowenthal, 1964; Scotch & Richardson, 1966; Tallmer & Kutner, 1970, Center for the Study of Aging & Human Development, 1978). But Havighurst (1973) found the lower class to have the most visiting with neighbors and kin. However, Havighurst agrees with Cutler (1976a) that upper SES persons are more active in voluntary associations. The most recent nationwide survey (Harris, 1975) found little difference between income or education groups in terms of their social and family involvement scale; but the *middle* income group and those with *least* education had somewhat higher involvement than others. Whites have been found to have more social activity than blacks (Harris, 1975; Center for the Study of Aging & Human Development, 1978), probably because whites tend to have higher SES on the average.

The relationship of sex to social activity is also ambiguous. The Kansas City study found more men to have a "large life-space" (a high number of reported monthly contacts with others, [Cumming & Henry, 1961] and the Texas study found men to have more "development" leisure activities (outdoor activities, travel, and organizational activity) and less solitary activities than women (Gordon & Gaitz, 1976). On the other hand, Harris's national survey (1975) found women to have slightly more social involvement.

Thus, the previous research agrees that being healthy, married, and living with someone tends to increase social activity; whereas the influence of SES and sex depends on where and how the study was done. However, there are two major limitations to most of this research. The first is its cross-sectional nature so that we do not know whether the factor (such as health) caused social activity or the social activity caused the factor. The second problem is that it tends to be bivariate or at most trivariate analysis. The several relevant factors involved in social activity are not *simultaneously* analyzed to see what independent effects they have when the other factors are taken into account.

We now turn to data from the Duke longitudinal studies which overcome these limitations.

The Duke Longitudinal Studies

We will examine the factors influencing social activity in two ways. First we will analyze the simple (zero-order) correlations of round 1 predictors of round 2 social activity. This is a bivariate longitudinal analysis which will give us information on which factors have any significant predictive association with any of the social activities. Second, we will examine a residual change analysis of which factors in the first round predict a *change* in social activity by the second round.

Table 4-2. *Significant* round 1 predictors of round 2 social activity, by sex (simple correlations).*

Predictors	Primary group contacts		Secondary group contacts		Religious activities	
	Men	Women	Men	Women	Men	Women
Age				−.21		−.28
Race (black)						.28
Mental function	.24		.30	.51	−.38	
Education			.22	.51	−.28	
Occupation (nonmanual)			.30	.47	−.34	
Physical function				.25	−.28	
Employment				.26		
Live with others	.41	.66				

Note.—Men = 92; women = 90.
* All predictors shown were significant at .05 level.
Source. First longitudinal study.

This is a multivariate longitudinal analysis and gives us information on which factors *influence later social activity* when initial levels of activity and other significant factors are held constant.

The first longitudinal study. In the first Duke longitudinal study we analyzed the associations of ten factors with three measures of social activity. The ten factors included three demographic variables thought to influence social activity: sex, age, and race. They also included three socioeconomic variables thought to influence social activity: mental function (the Wechsler Adult Intelligence Scale, full-scale weighted score), education (highest year completed), and occupation (coded 0 for manual, 1 for nonmanual.)* There were also two measures of health: the physical function rating and the health self-rating. Finally, there were two social environment measures that may influence social activity: employment and live with others (alone =1, live with others =2).

The three measures of social activity were primary group contacts, secondary group contacts, and religious activity.

The correlation matrix in Table 4-2 presents the simple (zero-order) correlations of significant round 1 predictors of round 2 social activity separately for men and women. Table 4-3 presents the unstandardized *b* weights and the variance explained (R^2) by the significant predictors of change in social activity from round 1 and 2. The *b* weight is the number of units the social activity measure changes for each unit change in the predictor. If change in a given social activity had no statistically significant predictors, it does not appear in the table.

These tables show that primary group contacts were primarily influenced by whether or not the man or the woman lived in a household with someone else. Living with others predicted more group contacts and a maintenance of group contacts over time. For women, being employed also predicted a maintenance of primary group contacts.

*Codes for all variables are given in the Appendix.

Table 4-3. *Significant* predictors of change in social activity from round 1 to round 2, by sex.*

Predictors	b	R^2
Primary group contacts: men		
Primary group contacts (rd.1)	.27	.17
Live with others	2.04	.20
Primary group contacts: women		
Primary group contacts (rd.1)	.31	.42
Live with others	2.53	.48
Employment	.62	.51
Secondary group contacts: women		
Secondary group contacts (rd.1)	.65	.50
Employment	.59	.56
Mental function	.01	.59

Note.—Men = 92; women = 90.
* All predictors shown were significant at .05 level.
Source. First longitudinal study.

Secondary group contacts were primarily influenced by such socioeconomic factors as education, occupation, and mental function: higher SES predicted more secondary group contacts for both men and women. In addition, employment also predicted more secondary group contacts for women. But women had more decline in secondary group contacts than men.

Religious activity negatively related to SES and to physical function among the men: apparently lower status and less healthy men were more likely to engage in more religious activities. Among women, younger age and being black was predictive of more religious activity. Thus, while much of religious activity involves secondary group contacts, SES is related in opposite ways to these social activities: positively to secondary group contacts, but negatively to religious activity (at least among the men).

In general women reported more leisure activity, religious activity, and secondary group activity, while men reported more primary group activity than women. This later finding may reflect the fact that fewer men were living alone.

The second longitudinal study. In the second study we analyzed seventeen potential predictors and four indicators of social activity.* The seventeen predictors included the two standard demographic variables age and sex, and four measures of socioeconomic status: education, mental function, occupation, and income. There were two health measures: physical function and health self-rating. Aspects of the environment were measured by the indicators, employment and number in the household. "Number of children nearby" was the number of children living outside the household but within a half-hour travel: while "number of nearby relatives" was the number of relatives living outside the household but within a half-

*Coding and other information about all variables may be found in the Appendix.

Table 4-4. *Significant* round 1 predictors of round 2 social activity, by sex (correlation matrix).*

Predictors	Total social hours		Visiting hours		Church meetings		Nonchurch meetings	
	Men	Women	Men	Women	Men	Women	Men	Women
Mental function		.20		.17		−.15	.25	.22
Education	.16	.18		.19		−.19	.29	.21
Occupation (nonmanual)	.16						.24	.17
# In household				−.14				
Income	.20					−.21	.39	.25
# Children				.14			−.13	−.14
Old identification							−.15	
Achievement values		−.15				.14	−.15	−.14
Internal control	.18						.14	

Note.—Men = 227; women = 216.
* All correlations shown were significant at .05 level.
Source. Second longitudinal study.

hour travel. There were also five social-psychological variables which are thought to influence social activity: old age identification, achievement values, internal control, busy, and respected.

The four social activity measures presented in these tables include total number of social leisure hours per week, number of visiting hours per week, number of church meetings attended per month, and number of nonchurch meetings attended per month.

One of the strongest and most consistent predictors of more social activity was being female: women reported about three more social hours per week than did men. They were consistently more active in visiting hours, meeting hours, and number of nonchurch meetings. They also tended to maintain their social activity over time more than men.

The total number of social hours were primarily related to higher socio-economic status among both men and women (Table 4-4 and 4-5). In addition, internal control orientation, among men, predicted more social hours and less decline in social hours; while a higher score on achievement values predicted slightly *fewer* social hours among women.

Number of visiting hours, which is a kind of primary group activity, was also related to SES variable among women. In addition, having fewer relatives inside the household but more children outside the household predicted more visting hours among women.

As in the first longitudinal study, SES was related to church meetings and nonchurch meetings in opposite ways: higher SES predicted fewer church meetings and more nonchurch meetings. Having more children outside the home predicted fewer nonchurch meetings for both men and women and a decline in church meetings among men. Perhaps children outside the home and nonchurch meetings are in some competition with each other. Identifying oneself as old or elderly also

Table 4-5. *Significant* predicators of change in social activity from round 1 to round 2, by sex.*

Predictors	b	R^2
Total social hours: men		
Total social hours (rd.1)	.71	.26
Internal control	.45	.28
# Church meetings: men		
# Church meetings (rd.1)	.77	.51
# Children	−.34	.53
# Church meetings: women		
# Church meetings (rd.1)	.67	.42
Income	−.04	.44
# Nonchurch meetings: men		
# Nonchurch meetings (rd.1)	.69	.42
Income	.08	.45

Note.—Men = 227; women = 216.
* All predictors significant at .05 level.
Source. Second longitudinal study.

predicted fewer nonchurch meetings among the men. Apparently those who thought of themselves as younger tended to go to more such meetings.

Consequences of Social Activity

In this section we are concerned with three possible consequences of social activity: health, happiness, and longevity. In other words, does social activity contribute to better health, more happiness, and longer life?

Previous Research

We have already reviewed the evidence showing an association between better health and more social activity. The unresolved question is the old "chicken and egg" question: to what extent does health cause social activity and vice versa? There is probably no certain way to resolve this question without carefully controlled experiments. There are good theoretical reasons to believe that the two factors are mutually reinforcing. Good health probably makes possible a greater amount of social activity. We know that most illnesses and disabilities tend to reduce social interaction by restricting mobility, reducing energy available, and interfering with communication processes. On the other hand, greater social activity probably tends to maintain health by stimulating more physical and mental activity, by providing a social network to help recovery from illness and to provide information and advice on health matters, and by maintaining a sense of self-esteem and social worth which contributes directly to better mental health and indirectly to better physical health.

The second possible consequence of social activity, happiness, is related to a large body of theory and research known as the disengagement *vs*. activity controversy. Disengagement theory has become rather complex, with hypotheses involving the inevitability and universality of physical, psychological, and social decline, increasing preoccupation with self-centered concerns, and societal withdrawal from aging persons. However, a major hypothesis of the theory, with which we will be concerned, states that disengagement from social activity in old age tends to result in the maintenance or reestablishment of higher morale (Cumming & Henry, 1961). In contrast, activity theory hypothesizes that maintenance of social activity tends to maintain morale while reduction of social activity tends to reduce morale (Lemon et al., 1972).

This basic hypothesis of disengagement theory has become hedged about with so many qualifications and escape clauses that it has become difficult to test. For example, it has been modified to state that disengagement maintains morale only when disengagement is voluntary; that forced disengagement causes lowered morale. This leaves the difficult empirical question of when disengagement is truly voluntary. It may be that the majority of disengagement is forced in one sense or another: by lack of money, health, or opportunity. In that case, disengagement would not result in higher morale for the majority of aged, and yet the theory could still claim validity for the minority who voluntarily disengage.

Another modification is that continued activity may maintain morale for the earlier part of old age, but that disengagement is sooner or later inevitable and will become best for morale among the very old. This leaves open the possibility that disengagement theory might be applicable to only the very old. Another problem with testing this theory is that when the aged are examined cross-sectionally, many aged may *appear* disengaged and still have high morale, but this is because they have had little social engagement all their lives, not because they have reduced social activity in old age. We have already indicated that there is considerable evidence for continuity in social activity.

Nevertheless, many studies have tried to test these hypotheses. Most of the studies agree that higher social activity tends to be associated with morale or life satisfaction; thus supporting the activity hypothesis rather than the disengagement hypothesis. For example, two early studies found that those aged with high personal adjustment tended to spend more time in social activities and voluntary organizations (Burgess, 1954; Lebo, 1953). Two other early studies found that those with more social activity had higher morale (Kutner, 1956; Reichard et al., 1962). A Chicago study found that activity became more important with increasing age for predicting life satisfaction (Tobin & Neugarten, 1961). An international study of six nations found substantial positive correlations between total activity in 12 social roles and life satisfaction (Havighurst et al., 1969). This was also found to be true among Chicago teachers and steelworkers. Another Chicago study found high morale among 72 percent of the aged with no major role loss, but only 30 percent of those with three or four major role losses (Rosow, 1967). Similarly Phillips (1957) found more maladjustment among those with role losses than those without.

However, a few studies found no confirmation of either theory or found that activity theory held only under certain circumstances. In a New York study, no confirmation was found for the disengagement hypothesis of high moral among the highly disengaged (Tallmer & Kutner, 1970). In San Francisco, interaction with a confidant appeared to be more important for high morale than the total frequency of all interactions or the maintenance of all social roles (Lowenthal & Havens, 1968). Also they found that reduction in social activity was associated with low satisfaction only if the reduction was caused by an externally imposed deprivation such as poor health, widowhood, or forced retirement (Lowenthal & Berkman, 1967). This fits the modification mentioned above that disengagement results in higher morale only when it is voluntary. A study of migrants to a retirement community found that only informal friendships correlated significantly with life satisfaction. General activity, relations with relatives, neighbors, and formal organizations had little or no correlations with life satisfaction. It should be noted that this study was based on a rather limited sample: white, upper-middle class migrants to a retirement community.

Three recent studies all agree that participation in voluntary organizations is unrelated to life satisfaction once health, income, and education are controlled (Bull & Aucoin, 1975; Cutler, 1976b; Ward, 1979). In other words, the apparent relationship between participation in voluntary associations and higher life satisfaction seems to be primarily caused by the better health, income, and education of the participants. On the other hand, the correlations of better health and SES with both voluntary organization participation and life satisfaction does not necessarily mean that the correlation of voluntary organization participation and life satisfaction is spurious. There may be real causal relationship between these latter two variables which is obscured when health and SES is controlled.

Previous reports from the first longitudinal study have reported that most participants fit the activity hypothesis: either consistently below the mean on both social activity and life satisfaction, although 14 percent fit the disengagement hypothesis of low activity combined with high satisfaction (Maddox, 1970). It was also reported that extreme increases or decreases in activity between the first two rounds tended to be accompanied by corresponding increases or decreases in life satisfaction.

The only study that has presented any evidence to support the general applicability of the disengagement hypothesis was the Kansas City study done by the originators of the disengagement theory (Cumming & Henry, 1961).

As for the consequences of social activity for longevity, one study of normal aged males found that a variable called "highly organized behavior" was one of the strong and significant predictors of survival (the other predictor was avoidance of smoking [Bartko et al., 1971]). "Highly organized behavior" was a five-point rating scale ranging from "few activities" to "many activities: structured, planned, varied, involved, new, complex, and self-initiated." Thus, those with many structured and organized acitivites (which would include social activities) had a substantially better survival rate.

Table 4-6. *Significant* round 1 activity predictors of round 2 consequences, by sex.*

	Consequences			
	Physical function		Happiness rating	
Predictors	Men	Women	Men	Women
Leisure activity	.32	.34		.32
Secondary group contacts	.25	.31	.20	.28

Note.—Men = 92; women = 90.
*All correlations shown were significant at .05 level.
Source. First longitudinal study.

Table 4-7. *Significant* activity predictors of change in consequences, by sex.*

Predictors	b	R^2
Physical function: women		
Physical function (rd.1)	.45	.27
Secondary group contacts	.12	.32
Happiness rating: women		
Happiness rating (rd.1)	.42	.31
Leisure activity	.11	.34

Note.—Men = 92; women = 90.
* All predictors significant at .05 level.
Source. First longitudinal study.

The Duke Longitudinal Studies

There was evidence from both longitudinal studies that more social activity tends to predict better health, happiness, and longevity. Three kinds of analysis show this: correlations of round 1 activity with round 2 measures of health and happiness; residual change analysis of round 1 activity with change in health and happiness; and correlations of social activity with greater longevity when other factors are controlled.

The first longitudinal study. The analysis of the correlations between round 1 activities and round 2 health and happiness show that for both men and women more leisure activity and more secondary group contacts significantly predict better physical funtion and higher happiness ratings (Table 4-6). Other measures of social activity were also positive predictors of health and happiness, but the correlations did not reach statistical significance.

The residual change analysis showed that at least among women, more secondary group contacts and more leisure activity significantly predicted positive change in physical function and happiness ratings (Table 4-7). The same relationships occured among the men, but the correlations did not reach statistical significance.

Table 4-8. *Significant* round 1 activity predictors of round 2 consequences, by sex (correlation matrix).*

| | Consequences | | | |
| | Health self-rating | | Affect balance | |
Predictors	Men	Women	Men	Women
Visting hours				.19
Meeting hours			.15	.19
Total social hours				.29
Nonchurch meetings		.15	.13	.22
#People seen	.15		.13	

Note.—Men = 227; women = 216.
* All correlations shown were significant at .05 level.
Source. Second longitudinal study.

Table 4-9. *Significant round 1 activity predictors of change in consequences.*

Predictors	b	R^2
Health self-rating: women		
Health self-rating (rd.1)	.60	.37
Total # meetings	.06	.39
Affect balance: men		
Affect balance (rd.1)	.40	.09
#People seen	.21	.11
Affect balance: women		
Affect balance (rd.1)	.58	.24
Social hours	.14	.29
#People seen	.30	.31

Note.—Men = 227; women = 216.
* All predictors significant at .05 level.
Source. Second longitudinal study.

The Second Longitudinal Study. The correlations between round 1 social activities and round 2 health and happiness showed several significant positive associations, especially among women (Table 4-8). More nonchurch meetings predicted better health among women, and more people seen significantly predicted better health among the men. Among both men and women more visiting hours, meeting hours, total social hours, nonchurch meetings, and people seen, tended to significantly predict and higher affect balance (more happiness).

The residual change analysis showed that more meetings attended significantly predicted an increase in health among women, more people seen significantly predicted an increase in affect among men, and both more social hours and people seen significantly predicted an increase in affect among women (Table 4-9). Other activity predictors of change in health and happiness were positive, but not statistically significant.

Table 4-10. *Significant predictors of longevity difference, by age.*

Predictors	r	b	R²	p
Men				
Age	.12	.06	.02	.35
Physical function	.31	1.07	.15	.01
Work satisfaction	.28	1.17	.19	.01
Employment	−.12	−2.11	.22	.01
No cigarettes	.20	2.82	.27	.01
Secondary group contacts	.24	.64	.29	.05
Women				
Age	.26	.24	.07	.01
Physical function	.26	1.44	.18	.001
Happiness rating	.31	.69	.21	.05

Note.—Men = 119; women = 109.
Source. First longitudinal study.

Thus, all these analyses tend to support the activity theory that more activity leads to better health and more happiness.

Predictors of longevity. In order to find if social activities had any consequences for longevity, we did a multiple regression analysis of possible predictors of the longevity difference (LD, see chapter 1).

One surprising finding was that although the LD is designed to control for age differences in life expectancy, there is a positive correlation between age and the LD in our sample: a small and nonsigificant correlation for men, but a larger and significant correlation for women. This means that the older participants in our study, especially among the women, were above average in terms of longevity (and/or younger participants were below average). Apparently the selection process in the first longitudinal study tended to select more elite persons, at least in terms of longevity, in the older age categories. However, the over-all average LD was just about zero, which indicates that the average participants survived just about as long as expected. Because we wanted to control for this difference between age groups, we entered age as a first control variable in the multiple regression analysis, even though it was not statistically significant among the men.

After age was entered, physical function was the strongest predictor of longevity among both men and women (Table 4-10). This simply indicates that healthier people live longer, as would be expected. Also as expected, avoiding cigarettes contributes to longevity. Of more interest is the fact that among men work satisfaction and secondary group contacts were significant predictors of greater longevity, even after health and all other significant variables were controlled. This indicates that social activites in secondary organizations can contribute to longevity—at least among men.

While the women had small correlations between secondary group contacts, leisure activities, and the LD, none of these were significant. But "happiness rating" was a significant predictor of LD among women even after health was controlled. Apparently, a more positive and optimistic attitude toward life tended to increase longevity among the women.

It is suprising that employment had a negative correlation with LD among the men, but the correlation became significant only in the multiple regression after age, health, and work satisfaction had been controlled. This seems to mean that unless one derives some satisfaction from work, employment is not beneficial and may reduce longevity. Apparently persons who have to work out of necessity and derive no satisfaction from it tend to die earlier than expected. In other words, satisfying work tends to increase longevity, but unsatisfying work tends to reduce longevity.

Summary

Although most previous studies tend to agree that social activity tends to decline with age, some types of social activity appear not to decline with age. Contacts with friends and relatives appear not to decline until the 80s. Participation in voluntary organizations tends to be stable or to increase until the 80s, when socioeconomic status is controlled. This is true of religious and political activity as well.

Both of the Duke Longitudinal Studies agree with the previous studies that total social activity tends to decline for both men and women, for the middle aged, the young-old, and the very old. However, there is considerable variation in social activity within the groups at any one point in time and in the amount and direction of change over time. There are substantial minorities who maintain or increase their social activity as they age.

As for specific types of social activity, both studies indicated gradual decreases in interactions with family and friends, but participation in organizations presented a mixed picture. There seemed to be no substantial changes in ratings of participation in organizations or hours spend in meetings. But a majority of the men in the first longitudinal study reported less club activity "now compared to age 55." Church activities tended to increase in late middle age and then decrease in late old age.

On the issue of increasing homogeneity vs. heterogeneity, previous research has presented evidence and theory on both sides. The evidence from the Duke studies does not support either side. The participants tended to maintain, but not to increase or decrease, their individual differences as they aged.

Both studies show strong evidence of continuity in the social activity variables. Usually more than half of the variance in any given variable can be explained by the scores on that variable in the previous round. As the interval between measures increases, the correlations decrease and most persons showed some fluctuation in at least one round, but most persons tend to maintain their approximate rank-order relative to others throughout most of the study.

As for the antecedents of social activity, previous research agrees that being healthy, married, and living with someone tends to increase social activity; but the influence of SES and sex depends on where and how the study was done.

The longitudinal studies show that the significant antecedents of social activity vary depending on the type of activity. Primary group activities were more strongly predicted by living with someone. Secondary group activities were most strongly predicted by higher SES and by being a woman. However, religious activity was negatively related to SES among the men. In general, women had more leisure activity, religious activity and secondary group activity, while men had more primary group activity than women. This latter finding may be explained by the fact that more men were living with others, and living with others is the strongest factor in primary group activity. Most of these predictors also predicted maintenance of social activity in the residual change analysis which controls for initial levels of social activity.

We examined three possible consequences of social activity: health, happiness, and longevity. While previous studies have found associations between social activity and health, they had not been able to show which causes or precedes the other. We found that various forms of social activity were indeed predictive of better health: leisure activities and secondary group activities in the first study, and more people seen as well as more nonchurch meetings in the second study. Residual change analysis tended to show similar results.

The previous evidence on social activity and happiness was mixed: some studies found relationships and other did not. We found clear evidence that activity tends to maintain happiness in both studies. Happiness was predicted by more leisure activity and secondary group contacts in the first study among both men and women, and by more meeting hours, more people seen, more visiting hours, and a larger total of social hours in the second study. Many of these relationships were also supported by the residual change analysis. Thus, no evidence supported the disengagement theory of a negative relationship, and most of the evidence supported the activity theory that social activity contributes to maintenance of health and happiness.

Two previous longitudinal studies of aging have found that social activity contributes to greater longevity. Our first longitudinal study also found that work satisfaction and secondary group activity predicated greater longevity among the men even after health and other significant factors were controlled. Women's longevity appeared less influenced by social activities and more by a generally positive attitude toward life.

Chapter 5. Social Networks

In this chapter we move to a consideration of the numbers and types of people with whom elders interact. We use the image of a network because it reflects the connections between interrelated persons. The spouse and confidant are closer to the elder person and have stronger ties than others. The absence of such persons may critically strain the elder's social network or even represent a rent in the fabric of interactions. The network image also implies that persons interacting with the elder usually have ties with each other (a spouse is also parent of children, children are also siblings, etc.).

We will be examining two primary dimensions of social networks: *type* of relationship and *density*. The *type* of relationship focuses on which kinds of persons interact with the elder (spouse, confidant, child, relative, friend, neighbor). In this chapter we will not be examining more formal types of relationships such as with employers, business persons, and officials. The *density* of a network refers to the numbers of people with whom the person interacts; the greater the number, the denser the network.

We will first examine the age, period, and cohort effects on type and density of social networks, then the antecedents of type and density, and third the consequences.

Age, Period, and Cohort Effects

Are there typical changes with age in the type or number of persons elders interact with? Have there been changes in recent decades in the frequency of such interactions? How do later birth cohorts differ from earlier ones in these interactions?

Previous Research

Living with spouse or alone. In the total population there was a moderate trend toward a larger proportion of persons being married and living with their spouse from 1940 to 1960, followed by a decline to previous levels by 1977 (Table 5-1). However, among persons over age 55, there was a consistent trend toward a larger percentage being married and living with their spouse at all age levels and for both sexes (read across rows in Table 5-1). This trend cannot be explained by the historical trend (period effect) toward fewer persons living with spouse after 1960. Apparently, because spouses are living longer, more recent cohorts of elders are composed of greater proportions remaining married and with spouse. This cohort effect is even stronger among men (an increase of 20 percentage points among men 75+ from 1940 to 1977) because wives' longevity has been increasing more than husbands'. In addition to this cohort effect, there appears to be a fairly constant age effect that is stronger for women than men, because more women are widowed than men. Among women there is a drop of about 20 points each age decade (compare percentages along the diagonal in Table 5-1). Among men the drop is about 5

Table 5-1. *Percentage married and living with spouse by sex, age, and year.*

Age	1940	1950	1960	1970	1977
Men					
Total 14+	58	64	66	62	61
55-64	74	77	80	82	83
65-74	65	68	73	75	78
75+	47	49	54	56	67
Women					
Total +	58	62	66	57	56
55-64	60	62	63	64	67
65-74	39	41	43	44	47
75+	14	17	19	19	20

Source: U.S. Census.

Table 5-2. *Percentage living alone by sex, age, and year.*

Age	Men			Women		
	1960	1970	1977	1960	1970	1977
All ages	3	5	7	5	7	9
55-64	8	8	8	15	17	18
65-74	11	13	12	24	31	35
75+	15	18	20	26	44	47

Source. Estimated from U.S. Census data on number of primary individuals.

points in the first decade (ages 55-64 to 65-74) and then 10 points in the second decade (ages 65-74 to 75+). As a result of the greater mortality among husbands than wives, two-thirds of all men over age 75 are still married and living with spouse, but only one-fifth of women are still with spouse. Thus, this most basic part of most persons' social network is present for most older men, but missing for most women over 75.

This leads to the related question of what happens to widowed persons: do they tend to live alone or move in with relatives or others? Has the trend toward more remaining married and living with spouse reduced the proportion living alone? It appears that most widowed men do tend to live alone, because the decrease in proportion of men who are married and living with spouse in a given cohort (shown in the diagonals of Table 5-1) is almost equaled by the increase in proportion living alone (diagonals of Table 5-2). But among women, the increases in living alone are about one-fourth smaller than the decreases in married and living with spouse. This indicates that more widows move in with relatives or others than do widowers.

Regardless of these sex differences, the overall trend toward more persons remaining married and living with spouse has *not* resulted in fewer persons living alone. On the contrary there has been a general trend since 1960 toward more persons living alone, both among the general population and among elders (Table 5-2. Data not available prior to 1960). In the general population this is probably a result of the trend toward less frequent marriage and more frequent divorces. But today elders are choosing to live alone, probably because their health and financial situation now permit widowed persons to live alone. Opinion polls have shown that most older persons prefer to live in their own households as long as possible if they can afford to.

In addition to this general trend toward more living alone there is also a strong age effect which increases the proportion living alone among both men and women but especially among women. Finally, there seems to have been an unusually sharp increase between 1960 and 1970 in the proportion of women over 75 who are living alone. This may be partly a result of the movement to deinstitutionalize impaired elders, the majority of whom are women. Almost half of all women 75 and over were living alone in 1977, raising major problems for society given the frailties common in this group.

Others in the network. There are no national data that would allow us to examine trends in the interactions of elders with persons other than their spouse. The only national data that allow us to look at cross-sectional differences by age are the 1975 Harris survey.

That survey systematically asked each person whether he/she had contact with close friends, children, brothers and sisters, and parents. They also asked persons under 65 if they had contacts with grandparents (30 percent did) and asked persons over 65 if they had contacts with grandchildren (75 percent did). As might be expected, most of those under 65 had contacts with parents (70 percent), but few of those over 65 did (4 percent). There was also a shift away from contacts with brothers or sisters (91 percent for those under 65 compared to 79 percent for 65+). Both of these shifts are due mainly to the higher death rates among parents and siblings of elders compared to parents and siblings of younger persons. On the other hand, the proportion with close friends remained about the same, and the proportion interacting with children increased from 73 percent for those under 65 to 81 percent for those over 65. Thus, the *types* of persons in the social networks tend to shift *from* those in the older and current generations (grandparents, parents, and brothers and sisters) *to* those in the younger generation (children and grand-children). This is simply because as one ages the contacts with the older and current generations are more vulnerable to disability and death, while the number of those younger than one's self steadily increases.

However, despite these shifts in types of persons, the overall *density* of the social network (numbers of persons and frequency of interaction) remains about the same. Persons over and under 65 had almost identical summary scores of interaction with family and friends in the Harris survey (1975). Similarly, only a few more of the elders (12 percent) compared to those under 65 (7 percent) said loneliness was a very serious problem for them.

The Harris survey did find a small but steady decline with increasing age in proportions of the sample having a confidant: "someone you feel close enough to talk about things that really bother you." The proportion saying "yes" declined from 96 percent at ages 55-64; 93 percent at 65-69; 92 percent at 70-79; and 89 percent at 80 and over. Also as would be expected, the proportions naming their spouse or parent as their confidant declined while the proportions naming their children increased.

As for the controversy about whether men and women become more alike or different as they age, the evidence from social networks is mixed. It is clear that women's marital status becomes less like men's in that more women than men become widowed. Widowhood eliminates the main person in most married person's network and thus has profound effects on interaction with the rest of the network. On the other hand, men's social network becomes more like the majority of women in that the men retire and lose most of their interaction with fellow employees and employers. Most women in this age cohort had little employment and thus were more dependent than men on relatives and friends in their networks. When men retire they also become more dependent for interaction on relatives and friends and thus become more like women.

The Longitudinal Studies

Just as with the national data, the Duke Longitudinal Studies show that a higher percentage of men than women are married and living with spouses at all ages (Figures 5-1 and 5-2). However, there is an interesting change in the pattern of declines as persons move from early old age to late old age. In the earlier years (ages 50 to 75) there is a much sharper decline in the percent married and living with spouse among the women than among men (Figure 5-2); but in the later years (75+) men and women decline at about the same rate (Figure 5-1). Apparently the rate of decline among women levels off after age 75 because most are already widowed, and the men's decline accelerates as mortality among their spouses accelerates.

As for relatives and friends in the social network, the first longitudinal study did not record the number of relatives and friends throughout the study, but it did ask about satisfaction with contacts with relatives and friends. There were no significant or consistent differences between men and women in this regard. Nor was there a noticeable or consistent decline in satisfaction with relatives and friends. Similarly, the second longitudinal study showed no significant differences between men and women in numbers of children and relatives outside the household nor in numbers of friends. Although there was some decline in numbers of friends and neighbors, this tended to be balanced by increases in numbers of relatives and children outside the household, so that the total numbers in the social networks tended to remain steady on the average. Apparently, most men and women in both studies tended to maintain enough persons in their social networks to satisfy their needs as well as they had in younger years.

The second longitudinal study had a a series of detailed questions asking about the ages of members of the household of nearby relatives, of friends, and of neighbors. We wanted to find out whether older people tend to increase or decrease their interaction with younger people as they grow older. There are grounds for expecting either outcome. One might expect that older people tend to increase their

Figure 5-1. *Percentage married and living with spouse by sex and year.*

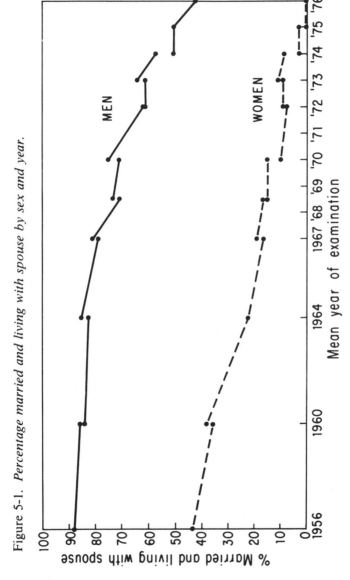

Note.—In rounds 1 and 2, *N* = 176; in rounds 10 and 11, *N* = 37.
Source. First longitudinal study.

Figure 5-2. *Percentage married by age cohort and sex (rounds 1 to 4).*

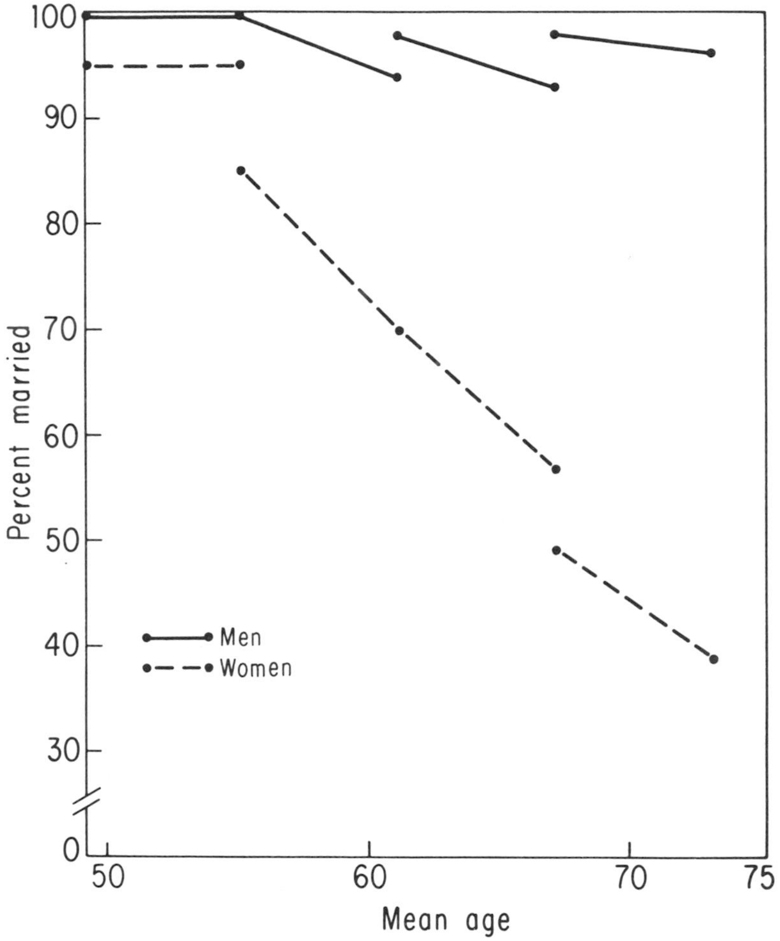

Source. Second longitudinal study.

interactions with younger people since a growing proportion of the people around them are younger. On the other hand, one might expect them to decrease their interactions with younger persons because of (1) general disengagement from the mainstream of society, (2) the "generation gap" which makes them feel uncomfortable interacting with younger generations, or (3) a growing "subculture of aging" which makes them feel they have more in common with their age peers (Rose & Peterson, 1965).

It turned out that when all persons in the social network are considered together (household members, children and relatives nearby, friends and neighbors), there was a slight (7 percent) but significant increase over the six-year interval in the pro-

Table 5-3. *Percentages of persons in social networks who were in a younger category than the panelist, by sex and round.*

	Household	Relatives	Friends	Neighbors	Totals
Men					
Total with any younger	182	118	175	174	187
% younger in round 1	35	25	52	47	50
% younger in round 4	28	66	45	50	57
p of difference	.05	.001	ns	ns	.05
Women					
Total with any younger	139	129	180	176	188
% younger in round 1	27	27	38	40	43
% younger in round 4	22	47	37	43	49
p of difference	ns	.001	ns	ns	.05

Note.—Categories of age were: under 45, 45-65, 65+.
Source. Second longitudinal study.

portion of persons who were younger than the study participant (Table 5-3). This was true for men and women. However, there was some decrease in the proportion of household members who were younger, presumably because children were moving out of the home. This was more than offset by the sharp increase in proportions of nearby relatives who were younger, presumably because grandchildren, nieces, nephews, and others in the younger generations were multiplying. There were no significant changes in the proportions of friends and neighbors who were younger. Thus, there is no evidence here of disengagement from the younger generation or of isolation of the aged in a "subculture of aging." On the contrary, this indicates that the proportion of the social network that is younger tends to increase as people age.

Antecedents

Previous Research

Living with Spouse. Almost all (over 92 percent) older persons are or have been married. And almost all older persons with living spouses, live with their spouse. Therefore the major determinant of whether an elder is living with spouse is whether they are widowed or not.

There are three well-known determinants of widowhood: age, sex, and socioeconomic status. There is a steady increase in widowhood with age, as shown in the previous section, because of increasing mortality rates. Furthermore, there is a decrease in remarriage rates with age, so that the older people are, the more likely they are to remain widowed. Second, there are substantially more widows among women then men for three reasons: (1) men have higher mortality rates than women, (2) husbands tend to be older than their wives and so have even higher mortality rates, and (3) widowers tend to remarry five times more often than widows do (Sheldon, 1958). The reason husbands have higher mortality rates than wives is uncertain, but appears to be due to a combination of genetic and life style factors.

Third, upper socioeconomic status (SES) persons are less likely to become widowed than lower SES persons. Here the major explanation appears to be differences in life style, although there may be some genetic influence (Palmore & Jeffers, 1971). Upper SES persons have all the advantages conducive to greater longevity: better nutrition, housing, and medical care; safer occupations; and generally greater resources for surviving crises. Blacks have higher mortality rates and therefore more widowhood (at least through age 75).

Children and relatives. Children are even more frequent persons in elders' social networks than spouses. Only half of all persons 65 and over have a spouse, but 79 percent have surviving children (Shanas, 1979). Also most elders with children see them frequently: over half have seen one of their children within one day, three-fourths have seen them within one week. Children are also the most frequent source of help for bedfast elders. About two-fifths reported that their children helped with housework or meal preparation, and two-thirds had children do shopping for them (Shanas, 1979). Even parents with children far away usually manage to see them on holidays and special occasions. But contacts with children are maximized if they live nearby (Atchley, 1977).

Elders from working class and lower SES groups are more likely to live with their children and to interact more frequently with them than those in the upper SES, according to Shanas's 1968 national survey. But Kutner in a 1956 New York City survey found the opposite: seeing children was more prevalent in high SES levels. Thus, evidence on the relationship of SES to interaction with children is conflicting in the previous research. However, parents tend to interact more with daughters than with sons, regardless of SES.

Interaction with relatives appears to be determined primarily by proximity and SES. Among working class elders it was found that geographic proximity was more important than geneological closeness in determining amount of interaction with relatives (Rosenberg, 1970). Also those with more income tend to interact with their relatives more often.

Siblings are the most frequent relatives (other than children) in the social networks. About four-fifths of elders have a living brother and/or sister (Harris, 1975), and over half of these have seen their siblings within the past month. There is some evidence that friendships between siblings tend to increase in old age (Lowenthal et al., 1975).

Grandchildren are the next most frequent relative; three-fourths report one or more grandchildren (Harris, 1975). Almost two-thirds of those with grandchildren report seeing them within the past month. Interaction and satisfaction with grandchildren is greatest when they are small children (Atchley, 1977).

Friends and neighbors. Almost all elders claim to have close friends and friendly neighbors, and their interaction with them is about as frequent as with children and relatives; in fact, it is more frequent than with any single category of children or relatives (Harris, 1975). However, those in higher SES groups report more friends and more interaction with them (Rosow, 1967; Kutner, 1956; Hunter

Table 5-4. *Significant* predictors of social network variables, by sex (correlation matrix).*

Predictors (round 1)	Social network variables (round 2)				
	Living with spouse	Living alone	Children contacts	Relative contacts	Friend contacts
Men					
Age	–	–	−.23	–	–
Race	–	–	.36	−.23	−.30
Education	.20	–	−.25	.25	.22
Occupation	.25	–	−.21	.26	.23
Physical function	–	−.26	–	.29	.28
Women					
Age	−.36	–	–	–	.16
Race	–	–	.27	–	–
Education	–	–	–	−.27	–
Employment	–	–	.24	–	–

Note.—Men = 92; women = 90. Number of friends were not available for round 2, so round 1 scores were used.
    * All predictors shown were significant at .05 level.
    Source. First longitudinal study.

& Maurice, 1953). Those who have lived in neighborhoods longer report more friends (Riley & Foner, 1968). Also those living in neighborhoods with a higher proportion of elders have more friends and interaction with them (Rosow, 1967). Finally, good health also facilitates more visiting with friends (Hunter & Maurice, 1953).

There is some evidence that women have more close friends, and men have more casual friends or associates (Clark & Anderson, 1967; Lowenthal et al., 1975). Part of this may be due to the fact that more women are widowed and thus need intimate friends to a greater extent and part of it may reflect our culture's sex role expectation that women will be more "warm" and "intimate" in their relationships.

The Longitudinal Studies

In both longitudinal studies we tested a series of possible predictors of social network variables. In the first longitudinal study we examined five social network variables: living with spouse, living alone, contacts with children, contacts with relatives, and contacts with friends. The possible predictors were sex, age, race, education, occupation, physical function, and employment.

As expected, the strongest predictor of living with spouse was sex: 88 percent of the men were living with spouse but only 43 percent of the women. But among the men those with more education and higher occupations were likely to be living with spouse (Table 5-4). This probably reflects the lower mortality rates among wives of upper SES men. Among women, age was a strong negative predictor of living with spouse, probably because of the increased mortality rates among husbands of older women.

Table 5-5. *Significant* predictors of change in social networks. (residual change analysis).*

Predictor	Change in	b	Increase in R^2
Men			
Occupation	Relatives contacts	31	.04
Race (black)	Children contacts	100	.09
Women			
Physical function	Living alone	−.06	.02
Race (black)	Children contacts	69	.04

Note.—Men = 90: women = 88.
* All predictors shown were significant at .05 level.
Source. First longitudinal study.

Living alone was also strongly related to sex: only 8 percent of the men, but 26 percent of the women lived alone. The only other significant predictor of living alone was physical function among the men: those with better physical function were *less* likely to live alone. Similarly, women with better physical function were *less* likely to move into the living alone category (Table 5-5). It is curious that although most of our participants appeared to have the minimal ability to function, the less healthy participants were those who more likely to live alone. Perhaps this is because the older persons were both in poorer health and were more frequently widowed.

Contacts with children were about the same for men and women. Older men had less contact than younger men, but age was not significantly related among women (Table 5-4). Among both men and women, blacks had more contacts with children. Also, blacks were more likely to maintain more contacts over time (Table 5-5). Similarly, the lower SES men had more contacts with children. This may reflect the larger families of lower SES persons, or it may reflect more family solidarity among blacks and lower SES persons.

In contrast, contacts with relatives and friends are *less* frequent among blacks and lower SES men (Table 5-4). This finding supports the research of Shanas and associates (1968) who found more interaction with children but less with other relatives and friends among lower SES groups. It may be that the limited transportation and other resources of lower SES groups limits much of their interactions to their immediate family (children), while the interactions of the upper SES groups are spread among relatives and friends, presumably because of their greater mobility. Health did not significantly affect women's social networks.

In the second longitudinal study we examined predictors of eight social network variables: living with spouse, number in household, having a confidant, number of children nearby but outside the household, number of nearby relatives, number of close friends, number of friends among neighbors, and total number in social network (Table 5-6). The predictors from round 1 we examined were sex, age, education, occupation, income, employment, and achievement values. We

Table 5-6. Significant* round 1 predictors of round 2 social network variables by sex (correlation matrix).

Predictor	Social network variable							
	Living with spouse	# In household	Confidant	# Children	# Relatives	# Friends	# Neighbors	Total network
Men								
Age	—	-.36	—	—	-.20	.13	—	—
Education	—	—	-.22	-.27	-.38	—	—	-.37
Occupation	—	—	—	—	-.26	—	—	-.15
Income	—	—	—	-.26	-.27	—	-.15	-.33
Employment	—	.17	—	—	.13	—	-.13	—
Achievements values (low)	—	—	—	-.14	-.17	—	-.15	-.24
Women								
Age	-.38	-.36	—	—	-.24	.18	—	—
Education	—	—	—	-.26	-.23	—	—	-.21
Occupation	—	—	—	-.18	—	—	—	—
Income	.50	.15	—	-.18	-.15	—	—	-.12
Employment	—	—	—	—	.30	—	—	.15
Achievement values (low)	.19	—	—	-.16	—	—	—	—

Note.—Men = 227; women = 216.
* All correlations shown were significant at .05 level.
Source. Second longitudinal study.

also tested several attitudinal variables such as external-internal orientation and feelings of self-respect, but none of them had any significant predictive relationship to the social network variables.

As in the first longitudinal study the strongest predictor of living with spouse was sex: almost all (97 percent) of the men were living with spouse but only two-thirds of the women. However, among women the strongest predictor of living with spouse was higher income; presumably because husbands in this age group are the primary source of income. Being younger also predicted living with spouse because of the increase in widowhood with age. High achievement values were moderately predictive of women living with spouse, but that relationship was not significant when age was controlled.

There was no difference between men and women in number in household, but it was strongly predicted by age in both sexes: older persons had smaller households as children moved out and husbands died. The other predictors became insignificant when age was controlled.

Having a confidant was somewhat more frequent among women (77 percent) than among men (66 percent). The only other significant predictor was that more educated men were less likely to have a confidant.

Men had somewhat more children nearby (1.0) than women (0.7), but both men and women with lower SES had more children nearby. This is similar to the findings in the first longitudinal study.

Men and women had about the same number of relatives nearby (3.8 and 4.0), and older age predicted less relatives nearby among both sexes. Presumably this is because some relatives die or move away as age increases. We have seen that persons tend to consider as close relatives and friends only those of a similar age to themselves, and this may explain the decrease with age of nearby relatives. Lower SES also predicts more relatives nearby among both sexes. Finally, employed men and women report more relatives nearby. This prediction persists even with controls for age and SES. It is unclear why being employed predicts more relatives but not more in any other category in the social network.

Men report somewhat more close friends (6.6) than do women (5.5). The only other significant predictor of friends was age: older men and women report somewhat *more* friends. It appears that the decline in household members and relatives was partially offset by the increase in friends with age.

Men also report a few more friends among neighbors (5.3) than do women (4.6). Employed men and those with higher income report fewer neighbors as friends, again perhaps because of less time to develop such friendships.

Summing up all these persons in the social network shows that the strongest overall predictors are the SES variables: those with lower SES have larger social networks among both men and women. The residual change analysis also shows that higher SES was predictive of decline in various measures of social network: higher education predicted decline in numbers of confidants and relatives among men, higher income predicted decline in numbers of children, friends, and total social network among men, and higher income predicted decline in relatives and total network among women. Predictors of maintenance of social networks among the men were health (more relatives) and perception of self as old (more neighbors).

Among women, predictors of maintenance of social networks were health (more children), employment (more relatives), and older age (more friends). This confirms the predictions from the correlation matrix (Table 5-6) discussed earlier.

Consequences

Previous Research

Spouse. There had been considerable research on the effects of loss of spouse in old age, especially through widowhood. Studies have found that persons without a spouse have lower morale (Gurin et al., 1960; Kutner, 1956), have lower incomes (U.S. Census), have higher rates of institutionalization (Palmore, 1976b), and higher mortality and suicide rates. Indeed, Holmes and Rahe (1967) assumed in the construction of their life events scale that loss of spouse would be the most traumatic of all events. Widows usually increase contact with their children, especially their daughters, and are more likely to move in with children (Shanas et al., 1968). They may also increase contacts with other relatives for a period, but then it usually diminishes (Atchley, 1977; Lopata, 1973). Widowhood's effect on friendships often depends on whether the friends are widows or not: widowhood tends to increase interaction with the former and decrease it with the latter (Atchley, 1977).

There has been considerable controversy over whether widowhood is more difficult for men or for women. Berardo (1968; 1970) has argued that it is more difficult for men, and Bell (1971) has argued it is more difficult for women. Atchley (1977) has made a review of these arguments and has concluded that widows *are* clearly worse off than widowers in terms of finances and prospects for remarriage, while widowers are not clearly worse off in any dimension.

In previously reported research, Heyman and Gianturco did not find any significant negative effects of widowhood among men or women in the first Duke longitudinal study (Palmore, 1974). Similarly, a recent analysis of the second longitudinal data found that widowhood produced a small drop in life satisfaction and increase in psychosomatic symptoms, but had no other measureable negative effects on health or adjustment (Palmore et al., 1979). We concluded that widowhood did not usually produce long-term serious negative effects on adjustment.

Children. Interaction with children often had equivocal effects (Blau, 1973; Rosenberg, 1970). If both parents and children are fairly healthy and independent, the interaction tends to boost morale; but if either becomes dependent on the other, there tends to be resentment, guilt, and conflict (Clark and Anderson, 1967). A recent large survey found no relation between frequency of interaction with children and morale of elderly parents (Lee, 1979).

As for the "empty nest" syndrome, there is no clear evidence that children leaving home produces any substantial negative effects. On the contrary, our previous analysis of the second longitudinal data showed that the last child leaving home tended to increase life satisfaction and affect balance (Palmore, et al., 1979).

Friends. Friendships clearly boost morale according to earlier studies (Blau,

1973; Rosenberg, 1970). Indeed, possessing a close friend or confidant has been found to be an important buffer against the trauma of reduced life space, widowhood, and retirement (Lowenthal & Havens, 1968).

The Longitudinal Studies

We systematically analyzed the possible consequences of the social network variables on health, happiness, and longevity. In the first longitudinal study we found no significant effects of the social network variables on health or happiness indicators, either in the correlation matrices or in residual change analyses. We suspect that our measures were not sufficiently sensitive to pick up the small effects that may have occurred.

We did find a few effects in the second longitudinal study. Among both men and women, living with spouse significantly predicted better health ($r = .15$). This might be partly due to the fact that those living with spouse tend to be younger and therefore healthier. However, in the residual change analysis that controls for initial level of health, living with spouse still significantly predicted better maintenance of health among men. This supports the theory that being married and living with spouse tends to maintain health, at least among men.

The only other significant zero-order predictor was number of friends which predicted higher affect balance among the women ($r = .26$). Furthermore, this prediction persisted when the initial level of affect balance was controlled in the residual change analysis.

The residual change analysis showed that number of friends also significantly predicts maintenance of physical function among both men and women. The sum of persons in the network also predicts maintenance of the health self-rating among men.

Finally, the number of children nearby significantly predicts maintenance of life satisfaction among women. This fits with the theory that children are more important to the life satisfaction of women than of men.

We also tested the social network variables to see if they would predict longevity in the first longitudinal study. None of these variables were significant predictors of longevity. Apparently the number and types of persons in social networks have no measureable effects on longevity.

Summary

There has been a consistent trend since 1940 among persons over 55 toward more in each succeeding age cohort being married and living with spouse. This cohort effect appears to be due to greater longevity, which reduces the frequency of widowhood in later birth cohorts. This trend is stronger among men than among women. However, the decline with age in proportions living with spouse is much greater among women than among men, at least up to age 75, because of the higher mortality of men.

Despite the long-term trend toward more living with spouse in each age group, there has also been a trend toward more elders living alone, probably because of improving health and finances.

With increasing age there is a shift *from* interaction with those in the older and contemporary generation (grandparents, parents, brothers and sisters) *to* those in the younger generations (children and grandchildren). This is probably because as one ages the number of persons older than oneself decreases while the number younger increases.

Men's social networks become more like women's when men retire and become more dependent on friends and relatives, but women become more different from men in that they are more likely to be widowed and thus lose interaction with a spouse.

However, the total number of persons in the social networks tended to remain steady on the average. There was some decline in numbers of friends and neighbors, but this was balanced by increases in numbers of relatives and children outside the household. Thus, despite shifts in the *types* of persons in the social network, the *density* tends to remain constant.

Furthermore, although the proportion of household members who are younger tends to decline, this is more than made up for by the increases in proportions of nearby relatives and neighbors who are younger. The result is an increase in the overall proportion of all persons in the social network who are younger. Thus, older persons do not tend to disengage from younger generations, although they no longer live in the same household with them.

There are three major determinants of living with spouse: age, sex, and SES. There is a decrease with age in living with spouse because of increased mortality rates and decreasing remarriage rates. More men than women live with spouse because women have lower mortality rates, wives tend to be younger than husbands, and widowers remarry more than widows. Upper SES persons live with spouse more frequently because of lower mortality rates.

Some previous research found that interaction with children was more frequent among lower SES and some found it more frequent among higher SES. Our longitudinal studies found that lower SES persons and blacks had more interaction with children. In contrast, the first longitudinal study found that lower SES men and blacks had less interaction with relatives and friends, while the second longitudinal study found that lower SES persons had *more* interaction with relatives and neighbors. Thus, the relation of SES to social networks remains ambiguous.

There was some evidence from the second longitudinal study that better health was predictive of the maintenance of social networks.

Previous studies have found that those living with spouse have higher morale, incomes, less institutionalization, and lower mortality rates. The second longitudinal study found that living with spouse predicted maintenance of better health, even after controlling for initial levels of health. Similarly, widowhood produced some decline in life satisfaction and some increase in psychosomatic symptoms. However, widowhood in the first longitudinal study had no measureable negative effects. It may be that widowhood is less traumatic among the older participants of our first study than among the middle-aged participants in our second study.

Children leaving home do not usually produce long-term negative effects. In fact, the second longitudinal study found that the last child leaving home tended to increase life satisfaction and affect balance. On the other hand, children living nearby predicted maintenance of life satisfaction among women.

Previous studies have uniformly found that persons with many friends had higher morale. Similarly, we found that more friends predicted higher affect balance among the women in the second study. Moreover, number of friends predicted better health among both men and women. However, social network variables had no significant relationship to longevity.

In summary, despite shifts with age in *types* of persons in social networks, most elders maintain the *density* of social networks. Also, having a spouse and maintaining friends predicts health and happiness.

Chapter 6. Sexual Behavior

Sexual behavior is sometimes thought to be irrelevant or inappropriate for elders. But as we shall see, this is a myth. Indeed, this chapter deals with a series of myths: that most older persons are asexual; that impotence and sexual problems in old age are irreversible; that those few who retain some sexual function suffer rapid declines; that an interest in sex by elders is abnormal or perversion; and that sexual activity in old age is dangerous or harmful. There are also the opposite myths: that older persons without sexual activity are abnormal or must be maladjusted and unhappy.

Aging Effects

Previous Research

The scientific study of aging and sexual behavior began with the Kinsey Reports (1948, 1953). These cross-sectional studies reported that although some sexual activity persisted among some persons late in life, there tended to be a general decline in all measures of sexual activity across the adult age range. This was true for both men and women, although the average women reported lower levels of activity than the average man at all ages.

The Kinsey Reports were flawed by a number of methodological problems (Palmore, 1952). However, subsequent studies have tended to support the Kinsey findings. For example, Freeman (1961) found that 55 percent of a sample of men with average age of 71 reported that they were sexually active. Similarly, Finkle et al. (1969) reported that 65 percent of older men up to age 70 indicate that they had engaged in sexual activity within one year. Masters and Johnson's clinical studies of the physiology of sexual response included several hundred men and women over age 50 (1966, 1970). Their discussions focused upon the factors associated with problems of sexual functioning in late life, but they concluded that maintenance of sexual function was normal among healthy, experienced, secure, rested, and temperate older men and women who had an available sexual partner.

However, these previous studies share several methodological problems which compromise the generalizability of their findings. One problem is the representativeness of the samples. Kinsey recruited community volunteers, drawing heavily upon the memberships of voluntary organizations. Such procedures are unlikely to generate representative cross-sections of the population. Finkle's subjects were clients of an outpatient clinic at a medical school and Freeman depended heavily upon referral of subjects from physicians and social workers. The first Duke longitudinal study also relied on community volunteers, but they were not recruited for participation in a study of sexual behavior and they were drawn from a larger sample of volunteers so as to represent the range of demographic variables in the community. The second longitudinal study was fairly representative sample of the broad middle SES groups in Durham.

Secondly, all the previous studies of sexual behavior were cross-sectional, with all the limitations of cross-sectional studies previously discussed (chapter 1). The effects of age are confounded with cohort membership and patterns of individual change over time cannot be examined.

A third problem is that prior studies have often not controlled for marital status. Patterns of sexual activity are strongly related to marital status, especially among women. Since widowhood increases in old age, lower levels of sexual activity in old age may be due to lack of a partner, rather than to lack of interest or ability.

The Duke Longitudinal Studies

The analyses presented here take into account these problems by (a) using more representative samples, (b) being longitudinal in design, and (c) including only persons remaining married during the period under analysis.

There have been a series of reports on sexual behavior based on the data from the Duke Longitudinal Studies. The first report was a cross-sectional analysis of married persons in the first longitudinal study, which found that there was no significant difference between age groups under age 75 in percent sexually active, but that those over age 75 had about half as many active (26 percent) as those under age 75 (54 percent) (Newman & Nichols, 1960). A second report on the first longitudinal study did some longitudinal analysis of the first two examinations (Verwoerdt et al., 1969). This analysis found that among married men about one-fourth were inactive on both rounds, about one-fourth were active and reported the same frequency on both rounds, one-third decreased activity, and one-sixth actually reported increases in sexual activity. Half of the married women were inactive, one-sixth had stable activity, one-fifth had decreasing, and one-seventh reported increasing activity.

A cross-sectional analysis of data from the second longitudinal study (Pfeiffer et al., 1972) found an overall pattern of lower sexual activity and interest in the later age groups, but they did not control for marital status. Only 6 percent of the men and 33 percent of the women said they were no longer interested in sex. Only 12 percent of the men and 44 percent of the women said they no longer had sex relations. However, by age 50 about half of men and women admitted they had noted some decline in their sexual interest and activity. By age 70, most men and women admitted such a decline.

The most recent report was on a longitudinal analysis of married persons in the second longitudinal study (George & Weiler, in press). It found small declines in each round in the mean level of sexual activity for the total group of married persons, as well as for each of six age-sex cohorts, although only one cohort had a decline large enough to be statistically significant (men initially aged 56-65). They also found that three-fourths had stable patterns of sexual activity over the six-year interval (including 10 percent with fluctuating levels), that one-fifth had decreasing patterns, and 6 percent had increasing patterns.

Figure 6-1 shows that between each pair of rounds in the first longitudinal study, married men and women tend to decline in the percentage with sexual relations. Among women this decline was from about one-half active in the early

Figure 6-1. *Percentage of married men and women sexually active* (rounds 1 to 5).*

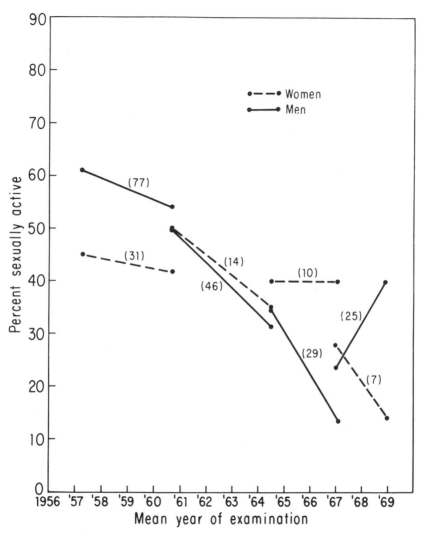

Note.—Ns in parentheses.
* *Sexually active* refers to those who report any intercourse.
Source. First longitudinal study.

rounds when their average age was in the upper 60s to about one-seventh active in round 5 when their average age was 77. Among men this decline was from three-fifths in round 1, when average age was 70, to about one-fifth when average age was 78. There were, however, two interesting exceptions to this pattern. Women had no decline between rounds 3 and 4, and men had an actual increase between round 4 and 5. This shows that even on the aggregate level some groups during some

Figure 6-2. *Frequency of intercourse among sexually active married men and women (rounds 1 to 5).*

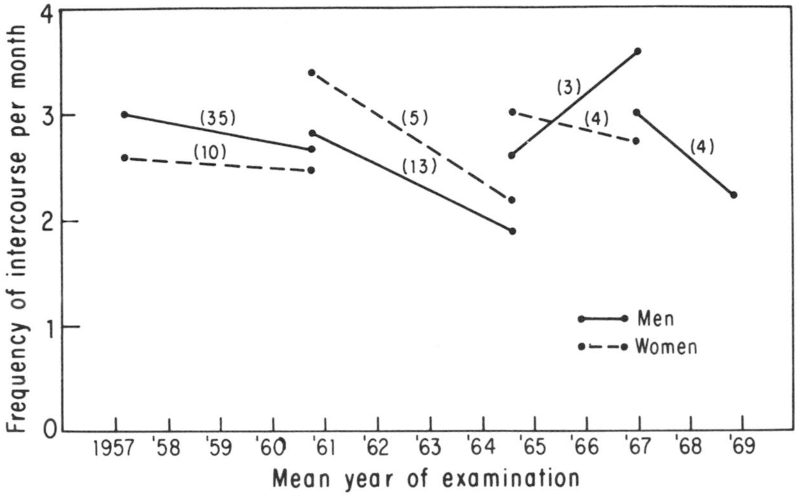

Note.—*N*s in parentheses.
Source. First longitudinal study.

periods have stable or increasing levels of activity. Furthermore, almost half of married women remained sexually active through their 60s, and about half of married men remained sexually active until their mid-70s. We will see that among healthy couples this proportion is much higher.

But even those who remained sexually active, there tended to be a decline in frequency of intercourse between each pair of rounds (Figure 6-2). Again there was one exception in that the three women who remained sexually active between the 3rd and 4th rounds reported an increase in frequency.

In the second longitudinal study, all of the married men in the youngest cohort (46-52) were sexually active at the beginnning of the study, but 5 percent became inactive by the end, six years later (Figure 6-3). Similarly, each of the male cohorts had a decline in percent active between the beginning and end of the study. Most of the female cohorts also had a decline. Also even the sexually active decline in frequency of intercourse (Figure 6-4). An even greater long term decline in frequency is shown by the fact that the average married man reported a decline from a frequency of 11 times a month when younger to about 4 times a month in round 1; while the average married women reported a decline from 8 times a month to 3 times a month.

However, such patterns of aggregate decline mask considerable variety in patterns of change on the individual level. In both studies, there were substantial proportions who reported stable or increasing sexual activity from earlier to later examinations. In the first longitudinal study 19 percent of the married men and 15 percent of the married women reported more frequent sexual relations in round 2

Figure 6-3. *Percentage of married men and women sexually active* by mean age for four cohorts (rounds 1 to 4).*

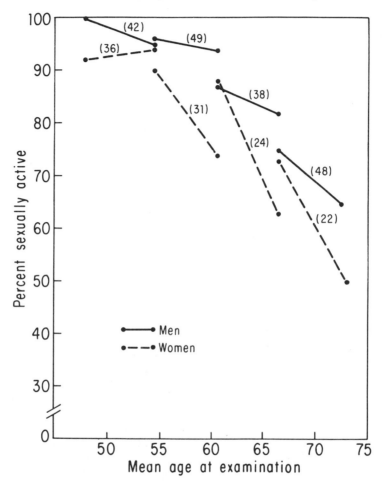

Note.—*N*s in parentheses. Each bar connects the percentage active in one cohort in rounds 1 and 4 for those present in both rounds.
* *Sexually active* are those who report any sex relations.
Source. Second longitudinal study.

than round 1 (Table 6-1). (The average age at round 2 was about 74 for the married men and 70 for the married women). We have restricted this analysis to married persons because we are uncertain about the validity of responses by the nonmarried. Nonmarried women report no sex relations, and many nonmarried men appear to be reporting on masturbation rather than on sexual intercourse.

In the second longitudinal study also substantial proportions at all ages report a higher frequency of sexual relations at round 4 than in round 1 (Table 6-2). There are relatively few who report no sexual relations and the modal pattern is one of

Figure 6-4. *Frequency of sex relations among sexually active married men and women by age cohort (rounds 1 to 4).*

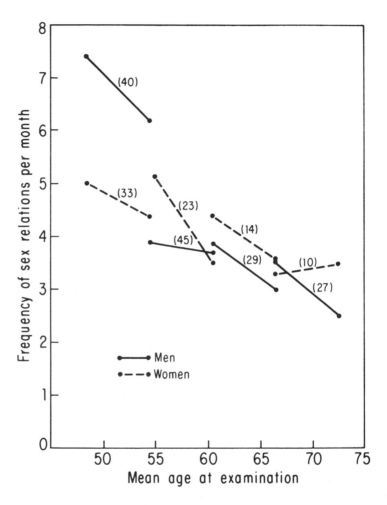

Note.—*N*s in parentheses. Each bar connects the mean frequencies of one cohort in rounds 1 and 4 of those reporting some sexual activity in both rounds.
Source. Second longitudinal study.

stability: the same frequency of sexual relations at both rounds. This is true even in the oldest cohort, those aged 70-75 at round 4, where a third of the men and women report stable patterns and about a tenth report increasing frequencies.

We have not presented the statistics on sexual interest and sexual enjoyment because they tend to follow the same patterns as the statistics on frequency of sexual relations: those with more frequent relations tend to report more interest and enjoyment. However, there are some who are no longer active for various

Table 6-1. *Patterns of sexual activity from round 1 to rounds 2 and 3 among married men and women.*

	N	No activity	Stable activity	Increase	Decrease
Men					
Rounds 1 to 2	77	37%	5%	19%	40%
Rounds 1 to 3	47	42	0	7	51
Women					
Rounds 1 to 2	31	54	4	19	27
Rounds 1 to 3	14	54	0	15	31

Source. First longitudinal study.

reasons but who report a continuing *interest* in sexual relations. The number with interest is always higher than the number who are active.

As for the issue of heterogeneity versus homogeneity, the standard deviations for frequency of sexual relations tend to decline for both men and women in both studies. This indicates increasing homogeneity as sexual activity declines.

Thus, these statistics show that most older married persons are not asexual; on the contrary, substantial proportions remain sexually active until at least their 80s. They also show that impotence and sexual problems in old age are reversible; and that substantial proportions at all ages report increasing sexual activity.

Antecedents

Prior Research

There has been no prior research on the antecedents of sexual behavior specifically among elders except for the Masters and Johnson studies (1966, 1970). However, there has been considerable research on the antecedents of sexual behavior among adults in general. The Kinsey studies established that women reported substantially lower levels of total sexual activity at all ages than men (Kinsey et al., 1953). This is true of married and unmarried persons. Our culture is a major cause of this difference between the sexes, but it is uncertain how much of this difference is influenced by biological differences.

Socioeconomic status does not seem to be consistently related to total sexual activity. The upper SES males had more masturbation, more nocturnal emissions and petting to climax; while the lower SES males had more premarital intercourse, more intercourse with prostitutes, and more homosexual relations. Higher SES females had more masturbation, and more frequent orgasms during coitus, but there were few other differences.

Religious devoutness was found to be a major factor restricting sexual activity of all types except marital coitus among both males and females of all ages. This was true among Protestants, Catholics, and Jews: the more devout were less sexually active in nonmarried outlets. Devout males also had 20 to 30 percent lower

Table 6-2. *Patterns of sexual activity* from round 1 to 4 among married men and women by age cohorts.*

	N	No activity	Stable activity	Increasing	Decreasing
Men					
46-51	42	0%	62%	9%	29%
52-57	49	2	63	16	19
58-63	38	8	58	8	26
64+	48	17	33	12	38
Total	177	7	54	12	28
Women					
46-51	36	6	61	17	17
52-57	31	10	45	7	39
58-63	24	8	42	8	42
64+	22	23	32	9	36
Total	113	11	47	11	32

* Sexual activity was measured by frequency of intercourse per month. The "increasing" category includes about 3 percent who changed from none to some, and the "decreasing" category includes about 10 percent who changed from some to none.
Source. Second longitudinal study.

frequencies of marital coitus, although this difference was not found among females.

Kinsey also found a marked cohort effect among women: those born in later cohorts were substantially more active in all forms of sexual outlet. Later cohorts of men engaged in less prostitute and more premarital and homosexual relations. Frequency of orgasm among women was substantially higher among those with premarital experience in orgasm.

Masters and Johnson studied sexual inadequacy among 150 women and 212 men age 50 and older (1966, 1970). They concluded that the best predictor of level of sexual activity in old age was the level of sexual activity in earlier years. They also found that the most significant social-psychological factors related to sexual inadequacy were: among women the absence of a secure and warm relationship with a socially appropriate male, and among men boredom, preoccupation with outside activities, fatigue, overindulgence in food and drink, illness of self or wife, and fear of failure.

The Longitudinal Studies

The earliest report on the first longitudinal study concluded that males and the lower SES persons had higher proportions sexually active. In addition, good health and being married were also strong antecedents of more sexual activity. A later report confirmed the importance of marriage on sexual activity, but pointed out that sexual interest tends to persist after marriage, especially among unmarried men (Verwoerdt et al., 1969). A third article reported that among the first longitudinal participants who had stopped sexual intercourse men tended to assign

Table 6-3. *Round 1 predictors of round 4 frequency of sex relations (zero-order correlations).*

Predictors*	Men	Women
Age	−.46	−.33
Physical function	.18	−
Health self-rating	−	.18
Education	−	.19
Income	.18	.21
Class identification	.15	−
Pleasure when young	.17	−
Frequency when young	.31	.44

Note.—Men = 178; women = 113.
* All correlations shown were significant at .05 level.
Source. Second longitudinal study.

responsibility to themselves, while women tended to blame their husbands (Pfieffer et al., 1968). A fourth report confirmed the same tendency among the participants in the second longitudinal study (Pfeiffer et al., 1972).

The fifth report analyzed the correlates of sexual behavior in the first round of the second longitudinal study (Pfeiffer & Davis, 1972). Among men the most important correlates of sexual interest and activity were past sexual activity, age, health, and social class (upper SES men were more active). Among women the most important determinants were marital status, age, and enjoyment of sexual activity in younger years.

When we analyzed the first longitudinal data to find what factors might predict later sexual activity, we found that only age predicted lower sexual activity ($r = -.20$ for men, −.37 for women). Neither objective nor subjective health, socioeconomic variables, happiness, nor prior sexual enjoyment significantly predicted frequency of sexual relations in round 2. This indicates that among married men and women at this advanced age, chronological age becomes the single important determinant of sexual activity rather than the factors that are determinants at younger ages.

Of course round 1 frequency of sexual relations was highly predictive of round 2 frequency ($r = .60$ for men and .77 for women). This shows that the rank order of frequency tended to be fairly stable over the four year interval between rounds 1 and 2.

In the second longitudinal study with its younger sample, there were a number of significant predictors of later sexual activity. Among men, age was still the strongest predictor, but round 1 health, income, class identification and pleasure in sex relations when younger had small but significant correlations with round 4 frequency of sex relations (Table 6-3). Frequency when younger had almost as high a correlation with later frequency as did age. Multiple regression analysis confirmed that age, frequency when young, and class identification had significant independent predictive power (Table 6-4). This significance of age and class persisted in a residual change analysis.

Table 6-4. *Round 1 predictors of round 4 frequency of sex relations (step-wise multiple regression analysis).*

Predictors	b	Beta	R^2
Men			
Age	−.22	−.44	.21
Frequency when young	.35	.25	.27
Class identification	.84	.18	.31
Women			
Frequency when young	.40	.43	.19
Age	−.14	.28	.26
Education	.20	.21	.29

* All predictors shown increase the variance significantly at the .05 level.
Source. Second longitudinal study.

Among women, frequency when younger had an even higher correlation with later frequency than did age (Table 6-3). The women also had small but significant correlations between round 1 health, socioeconomic status (education and income), and round 4 frequency. Multiple regression analysis showed that frequency when younger, age, and education, had significant independent predictive power (Table 6-4).

Thus, among both men and women chronological age and prior frequency of sexual relations were the two strongest predictors of later sexual frequency, but socioeconomic measures also were positive predictors of sexual activity. It is unclear why higher SES predicts more sexual activity: perhaps because higher SES persons in this age range are less inhibited than lower SES persons, or perhaps because higher SES persons tend to be healthier.

Consequences

Previous Research

There has been little or no direct research on the consequences of sexual activity for happiness, health, or longevity. It is well established that married persons tend to be happier, have better health, and live longer than single, widowed, or divorced persons. But there is no evidence as to whether this association is simply due to the selective nature of marriage (marriage selecting out those who would have been happier, healthier, and longevous anyway) or due to the security provided by marriage, or due to some other nonsexual factor.

Probably the most common assumption these days is that normal sexual activity contributes to happiness, health, and longevity. But there are still many who believe that sexual encounters lead to misery more often than not, that sexual activity is physically and emotionally exhausting and therefore unhealthy, as well as that promiscuous sexual activity spreads veneral disease and that strenuous sexual activity can cause heart attacks or other physical impairments.

The Longitudinal Studies

Because of this lack of prior research, the analysis of consequences of sexual activity in our longitudinal studies becomes especially important. In the first study we did correlation and residual change analysis with frequency of sex relations in round 1 as the predictor and with round 2 life satisfaction, happiness, health, and longevity as the dependent variables. There were no significant correlations among the women, probably because so few of the women were still sexually active (15 percent). However, among the men, both life satisfaction ($r = .20$) and health stability or improvement ($r = .28$) were significantly predicted by sexual activity. However, the residual change analysis showed no significant effects once initial levels of the dependent variables were controlled, probably because there was so little change in these variables between rounds 1 and 2. As for longevity, sexual activity had no effect one way or the other. Apparently sexual activity neither extends nor shortens life among this age group.

In the second longitudinal study we tested round 1 frequency of sex relations and decline of sex relations as predictors of round 2 physical function rating, health self-rating, psychosomatic symptoms, affect balance, and life satisfaction. We ran both correlation matrices and residual change analysis among married persons and for all persons, but Table 6-5 presents the results for married only so that the findings can not be interpreted as due to differences between married and non-married in both sexual activity and the measures of consequences.

Among the married men both round 1 frequency and no decline in sexual relations were significant predictors of both health measures and of affect balance. No decline was also a predictor of less psychosomatic symptoms. These symptoms can result from both poorer physical health and from greater neuroses or anxiety. Most of these consequences persisted in the residual change analysis. Among the married women there were less significant consequences but frequency did significantly predict physical function and negatively predicted psychosomatic symptoms, while no decline predicted better affect. The prediction of physical function by frequency maintained its significance in the residual change analysis. Thus, there are several indications that sexual activity tends to maintain or enhance both health and happiness among both men and women aged 45 to 70.

Summary

Previous research and the longitudinal studies agree that there tends to be a gradual decline with age in sexual activity. Part of this decline is due to widowhood, but even among married men and women there tended to be declines in the proportions who were sexually active. However, there were some exceptions to this general pattern in that some pairs of rounds in the first study and some age cohorts in the second study did not show a decline. This shows that even on the aggregate level, some groups during some periods have stable or increasing levels of activity.

Furthermore, almost half of married women remained sexually active through their 60s and about half of the married men remained sexually active until their mid 70s. Also, in both studies there were substantial proportions who reported stable or

Table 6-5. *Consequences of sexual activity for married men and women (correlation matrix*).*

Round 1	Round 2 consequences			
Sexual activity	Physical function	Health self-rating	Psychosomatic symptoms	Affect balance
Married men				
Frequency	.17	.20	–	.13
No decline	.22	.18	–.17	.17
Married women				
Frequency	.18	–	-.16	–
No decline	–	–	–	.20

Note.—Men = 216; women = 148.
* All correlations shown were significant to .05 level.
Source. Second longitudinal study.

even increasing sexual activity from earlier to later examinations. The statistics on sexual interest and sexual enjoyment tended to follow the same patterns.

Thus, most older married persons are not asexual; substantial proportions remain sexually active until at least their 80s; and substantial proportions at all ages report *increasing* sexual activity. However, there is increasingly homogeneity as frequency declines.

The only previous study of antecedents of sexual activity among elders concluded that the best single predictor of activity in old age was activity in younger. Similarly, we found that among both men and women in the second study, past frequency and pleasure in sexual relations were among the strongest predictors of sexual relations. Additional significant predictors of sexual frequency among both men and women were health and socioeconomic status; higher SES and healthier persons tended to be more sexually active.

Life satisfaction and health were both significant consequences of frequency of sex relations among men in the first study. Longevity had no apparent relationship to sexual activity. In the second study there were several significant indications that sexual activity tends to maintain or enhance both health and happiness among men and women. Thus, rather than being abnormal, dangerous, or harmful, this evidence indicates that sexual activity usually contributes to better health and happiness in later life.

Chapter 7. Life Satisfaction

Life satisfaction is the topic of this last chapter before the conclusions because I believe it to be among the most important, if not *the* most important factor in late life. Many consider it to be the primary ingredient in "the good life" and the ultimate criteria of "successful aging." Life satisfaction may also contribute to better health and a longer life. In this chapter the term *life satisfaction* usually refers to the general concept of subjective well-being, which may be measured by a variety of indicators and includes other concepts such as happiness and morale. There are, however, some specific scales that are life satisfaction indexes, such as total life satisfaction, happiness attitude, happiness rating, the life satisfaction ladder, the affect balance scale, the anomie scale, feeling useful, work satisfaction, emotional security, and prestige. (These indicators are identified and explained in the appendix.)

Because of the general belief in the importance of life satisfaction in aging, there has been much research on its relationship to age and on its antecedents. But all prior published research has been cross-sectional, which has made ambiguous the proper interpretation of the findings.

Aging Effects

Previous Studies

One of the most controversial questions in gerontology is whether growing older makes people more satisfied, less satisfied, or has no effect. There have been at least eighteen published studies within the past 25 years which have attempted to answer that question (Larson, 1978).

About one-third of these studies have found fairly clear *positive* relations between older age and more life satisfaction, and have interpreted this as resulting from a greater sense of achievement in later life, or from lowered expectations, or from the increased leisure and freedom from work and child-rearing, or from greater maturity and experience, etc. On the other hand, another third of the studies have found a fairly clear *negative* relation of age and life satisfaction. They have interpreted this as resulting from the loss of roles and status, reduced income, failing health, bereavement, and ageism in our society. The other third of the studies have found little or no relationship between age and life satisfaction.

How can we reconcile these divergent results? There are two possiblilties. First, the differences may be the result of different measures used. Most of the studies with positive findings between age and life satisfaction have used global measures of satisfaction with life as a whole (Cantril, 1965; Campbell et al., 1976; Lowenthal et al., 1975), but most of the studies with negative findings have used measures of current happiness, morale, or affect (Kutner, 1956; Gurin et al., 1960; Bradburn & Caplivitz, 1965; Bradburn, 1969; Clark & Anderson, 1967). Indeed, Campbell et al. (1976), found both a positive relation between age and life satisfaction as well as a negative relation between age and happiness. They conclude that older people are more *satisfied* with their life as a whole because of greater accomplishments and perhaps lowered expectations, but they are also less *happy* than younger persons because of lowered income, health, etc.

A second possible resolution of these discrepancies is based on when they were done. Most of the earlier studies, those prior to 1970, found negative relations between age and life satisfaction. Kutner in 1956 found a negative relation (*tau b* = −.11) between age and moral among 394 residents of Manhatten. Gurin in 1960 found a negative relationship between age and percent reporting they were "very happy" (a drop from 38 percent at ages 35-44 to 27 percent at ages over 55). Neugarten in 1961 found negative relations between age and life satisfaction scales (r = −.07 and −.10) among older persons in Kansas City. In 1967 Clark and Anderson found a strong negative relation (rt = −.20) between age and a satisfaction-depression scale among older residents of San Francisco.

But most of the studies published since 1970 have either found positive relations, no relation, or weak negative relations which become insignificant when socioeconomic status, sex, and other background factors are controlled. For example, there were three studies published in 1976 that reported positive relations. Lowenthal et al. (1975) found that preretirement couples had higher proportion reporting they were "very happy," having higher life satisfaction, and higher affect balance (the difference between positive and negative affect), in comparison with middle-aged couples. Campbell et al. (1976) reported higher life satisfaction at ages over 65 in a nation-wide sample. Kivett (1976) found higher happiness ratings among older participants in her study of North Carolinians.

Several studies since 1970 found no relationship between age and life satisfaction: Lawton's study of residents of homes for the aged (1972); Andrews and Withey's nationwide surveys of well-being among American adults (1976); and Spreitzer and Snyder's study of older Americana (1974). Two studies since 1970 found weak negative relations initially, but these tended to become insignificant when controls were introduced (Edwards & Klemmack, 1973; Larson, 1975). Harris (1975) is the exception, who found lower satisfaction among those over 65, but he did not use any controls for SES, etc.

This trend from negative findings in the early surveys to positive or neutral findings in later surveys suggests that there may have been a historical shift in the relation of age to life satisfaction. It may be that older persons have become more satisfied with their lives in recent years. We know that their relative education, income, and probably their health, has improved since 1970 (Palmore, 1976a). Perhaps the billions being spent on programs for the aged are actually improving their life satisfaction.

The difficulty with interpreting any of these findings is that they are all from cross-sectional studies and only show age differences rather than age-related changes. Thus, rather than reflecting the effects of aging they may reflect only sampling error between age categories, or cohort differences between successive generations. We turn now to the longitudinal studies which measure changes with age in the same group of people.

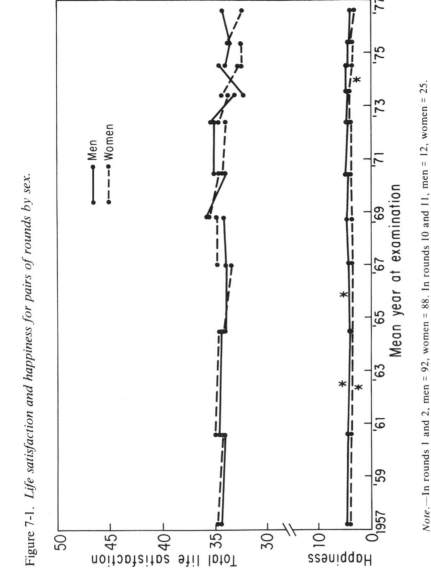

Figure 7-1. *Life satisfaction and happiness for pairs of rounds by sex.*

Note.—In rounds 1 and 2, men = 92, women = 88. In rounds 10 and 11, men = 12, women = 25.
* Indicates change was significant.
Source. First longitudinal study.

The Longitudinal Studies

In the first longitudinal study we analyzed changes in three indicators of life satisfaction: total life satisfaction, happiness attitude, and happiness rating. Figure 7-1 shows that there were little or no significant changes in either total life satisfaction or in the specific happiness attitude over the twenty years of the study.

Figure 7-2. *Change* in life satisfaction by age and sex cohorts (rounds 1 to 4).*

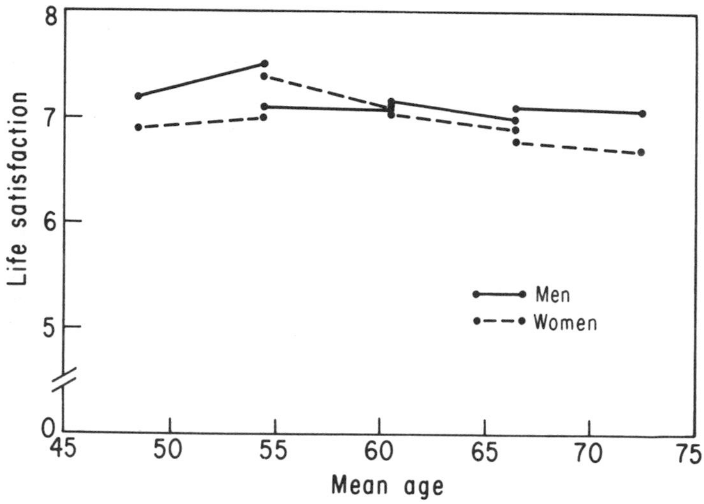

* No changes were statistically significant.
Source. Second longitudinal study.

There were a few statistically significant changes in the happiness attitude, but some were increases and some were decreases which tended to cancel each other out over time. The happiness ratings by the interviewer were more erratic, with a large number of statistically significant increases and decreases, but there also tended to cancel each other out so that the later scores were only about one point above the earlier scores. We suspect that even this difference is due mainly to differences between interviewers because of the erratic pattern of scores. Thus, there is no evidence for any consistent increase or decrease in life satisfaction from the first study.

The second study also included 3 measures related to life satisfaction: the life satisfaction ladder, the affect balance scale, and the anomie scale. Figure 7-2 shows that there were no significant changes among men or women in any of the cohorts in the life satisfaction ladder, although women showed a slight decline past age 55. Similarly, Figure 7-3 shows that while there were no significant changes in anomie among men, there were 2 significant increases in anomie among women. The anomie scale may be considered to be a negative indicator of life satisfaction because it is based on such items as "With everything in such a state or disorder, it's hard for a person to know where he stands from one day to the next" and "I often feel awkward and out of place." But it has a negative correlation with the life satisfaction ladder of only −.07 among men and −.12 among women, which indicates that anomie measures an independent dimension of psychological well-being.

The affect balance scale showed big increases from round 1 to round 2 and then erratic decreases to round 4. Since there seems to be no other explanation, we have

Figure 7-3. *Change in anomie by age and sex cohorts (rounds 1 to 4).*

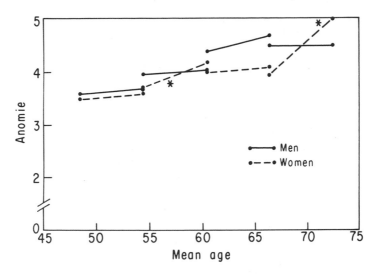

* Indicates change was significant.
Source. Second longitudinal study.

concluded that these fluctuations between rounds are mostly the result of differences in the way the scale was administered by the different interviewers in the different rounds.

Therefore, the general picture in both studies is one of remarkable stability in measure of life satisfaction, with some evidence that life satisfaction among women may tend to decline somewhat between the ages of 55 and 75.

As for the issue of increasing homogeneity or heterogeneity, we found no clear evidence for either one among the life satisfaction measures. The standard deviations for all these measures tended to remain stable or to fluctuate with no particular pattern.

Antecedents

Previous Research

Because of the widespread interest in life satisfaction as a major component of successful aging, there have been even more studies of its antecedents than of its differences among age groups (Larson, 1978). These studies have yielded a consistent body of findings.

The strongest correlate of life satisfaction is usually health or lack of physical disability. Fourteen major studies have found positive correlations ranging from .11 to .53, which explain from 1 percent to 28 percent of the variance in life satisfaction. The subjective measures of health tend to correlate with life satisfaction more highly than do the objective measures such as physician's rating. It appears that a person's health is less important to life satisfaction than is perceived health.

The second most important antecedent is usually socioeconomic status (SES). The same 14 studies found positive correlations between SES and life satisfaction ranging from .10 to .41, which explains from 1 percent to 16 percent of the variance.

The third important correlate of life satisfaction is social activity: more active elders tend to report higher life satisfaction. Seventeen studies agree that there are positive correlations ranging from about .10 to .46, which explains about 1 percent to 21 percent of the variance.

There is also some evidence that continued employment and being married (as opposed to being widowed or divorced) are related to higher life satisfaction; but these relationships tend to disappear when health and SES are controlled.

Several studies have found that improved or better housing is related to somewhat better life satisfaction (Carp, 1968; Lawton & Cohen, 1974; Martin, 1973; Schooler, 1969; Smith & Lipman, 1972). One study found the availability of transportation was significantly related to more life satisfaction even with controls for other factors (Cutler, 1975).

There appear to be no consistent or substantial life satisfaction differences between men and women, and occasional differences between whites and blacks disappear when controls for SES and health are introduced.

Despite this general agreement on the correlates of life satisfaction, since all these studies were cross-sectional, there is no way to determine which comes first and causes the other: the life satisfaction or the correlate. In the absence of longitudinal or experimental data, it is just as reasonable to infer that life satisfaction is a cause of better health and more social activity as to assume that it is an effect. Our longitudinal data allow us to examine both possibilities.

The Longitudinal Studies

In the first longitudinal study, the strongest predictor of life satisfaction among men was change in financial status: those whose financial status had declined had substantially lower life satisfaction than others (Tables 7-1 and 7-2). Notice that the *change* is more predictive of life satisfaction than the absolute level of current financial status. It appears the present income *relative to prior income* is more important to life satisfaction than is present income by itself. The second strongest predictor among men was sexual enjoyment: those with more sexual enjoyment reported substantially more life satisfaction (even after controlling for change in financial status, Table 7-2). The third significant predictor was health self-rating: healthier men had more life satisfaction (even after controlling for financial status and sexual enjoyment). Physical function rating (by the physician) was also positively related, but it was not statistically significant, which indicates that one's subjective evaluation of one's health is more important for life satisfaction than a physician's objective evaluation.

Among the women, change in financial status is somewhat less important, and total activity is most important: more active women report much higher life satisfaction. Also more important for women than men is the second predictor:

Table 7-1. *Significant predictors of total life satisfaction and happiness attitudes for men and women (correlation matrix).*

Predictors (round 1)	Life satisfaction (round 2)	Happiness attitudes (round 2)
Men		
Health self-rating	.22	.22
Employment	–	.22
Current financial status	.24	–
Change in financial status	.41	.20
Sexual enjoyment	.27	–
Total activity	.27	–
Women		
Health self-rating	.37	.21
Employment	.25	.28
Current financial status	.38	.27
Change in financial status	.33	.27
Intimate contacts	.21	–
Leisure activities	.39	.24
Religious activities	.22	.28
Total activity	.58	.46
Nonmanual occupation	.22	–
Performance intelligence	.24	–

Note.—Men = 92; women = 90.
* All predictors shown were significant at .05 level.
Source. First longitudinal study.

health self-rating. Several other factors had significant zero-order correlations with life satisfaction among women, but none of these remained independently significant after activity, health, and change in financial status were controlled (Tables 7-1 and 7-2).

The predictors of happiness were similar to those of life satisfaction, but the correlations tended to be lower for the predictors of happiness. One exception was that employment was a significant predictor of happiness (but not life satisfaction) among the men.

In the second longitudinal study we did not have a measure of change in financial status, but health self-rating and sexual enjoyment were again significant predictors of life satisfaction among both men and women (Table 7-3 and 7-4). Affect balance (a measure of happiness) was also significantly predicted by health self-rating among both men and women. In addition, several other predictors had significant zero-order correlations with affect balance among the women, but only health self-rating, social leisure hours, and sexual enjoyment were independently significant in the multiple regression (Table 7-5). We also examined predictors of anomie, which is a scale measuring attitudes of "normlessness," uncertainty, powerlessness, and goalessness. This scale had many significant predictors, but the strongest ones appeared to be related to socioeconomic status such as income,

Table 7-2. *Multiple regression of significant* predictors of life satisfaction.*

Predictors (round 1)	Life satisfaction (round 2)		
	r	R²	b
Men			
Change in financial status	.41	.16	2.43
Sexual enjoyment	.27	.21	1.92
Health self-rating	.22	.24	1.21
Women			
Total activity	.58	.34	.44
Health self-rating	.37	.39	1.47
Change in financial status	.33	.43	1.32

Note.—Men = 91; women = 85.

* Increase in variance accounted for by each predictor was significant at .05 level.

Source. First longitudinal study.

education, and intelligence (Tables 7-3 and 7-6). It appears that being in the lower socioeconomic groups tends to increase anomie, more than it decreases life satisfaction or affect balance.

When residual change analysis was done on these variables in the second study, health self-rating persisted as a significant predictor of change in affect balance among men and women; and social hours and sexual enjoyment persisted as significant predictors of change in affect balance among women. Education persisted as a significant predictor of change in anomie among both men and women.

Thus, health and sexual enjoyment were the two most consistent predictors of life satisfaction measures in both studies. In addition, change in financial status was the strongest predictor among men and total activity was the strongest predictor among women in the first study.

Predictors of successful aging. A special analysis was made of the predictors of successful aging in the first study (Palmore, 1979a). Successful aging was defined as surviving to age 75 in good health and happiness. More specifically, the criteria were surviving to age 75 with less than 20 percent disability and a happiness rating indicating generally or always happy, contented, and unworried. Only the 155 persons aged 60 to 74 at the beginning of the study were included in this analysis, and the predictors were taken from the first round so that the analysis would be a true prospective study. Seventy persons met the 3 criteria and were classified as successful aging persons, the other 85 were classified as not successful. On the basis of previous research and theory 18 variables from the first examination were selected for testing as predictors. Eight of the variables did not have significant correlations with successful aging: age, sex, marital status, education, performance intelligence, verbal intelligence, cigarette smoking, and primary group activities.

The two strongest predictors, as expected, were the physical function rating and the happiness rating. This simply reflects our general finding that the best single predictor of a score at a later point in time is usually the person's score on that

Table 7-3. *Significant* predictors of life satisfaction, affect balance, and anomie (correlation matrix).*

Predictors (round 1)	Life satisfaction (2)	Affect balance (2)	Anomie (2)
Men			
Health self-rating	.30	.24	–
Organizational activity	–	–	–.21
Social leisure hours	–	–	–.14
Internal control	–	–	–.17
Confidant	–	–	.22
Sex enjoyment	.14	.15	–
Verbal intelligence	–	–	–.56
Performance intelligence	–	–	–.47
Income	–	–	–.46
Education	–	–	–.49
Age	–	–	.15
Women			
Health self-rating	.20	.35	–.29
Physical function rating	–	–	–.15
Organizational activity	–	.17	–
Social hours	–	.29	–.21
Internal control	.14	.19	–.20
Sex enjoyment	.14	.25	–.25
Sex frequency	–	.14	–.26
Verbal intelligence	–	.27	–.53
Performance intelligence	–	.22	–.43
Income	–	.20	–.34
Education	–	.30	–.54
Age	–	–	.21

Note.—Men = 227; women = 215.
* All predictors shown were significant at .05 level.
Source. Second longitudinal study.

variable at an earlier point in time. Of more interest are the other 8 significant (zero-order) predictors: secondary group activities, physical activities, solitary activities, usefulness, work satisfaction, emotional security, prestige, and financial status. When these 8 variables were put into a multiple regression analysis, we found that for women the 3 strongest predictors were secondary group activity, physical activity, and solitary activity. For men the strongest predictors were secondary group activity, work satisfaction, and physicial activity. These findings support the activity theory of aging in that two of the strongest explanatory predictors of successful aging among both men and women were secondary group activity and physical activity, with work satisfaction also being important for men. This indicates that men and women who are more active in organizations and who engage in more physical activity are more likely to age successfully.

Table 7-4. *Significant* predictors of life satisfaction (multiple regression).*

Predictor	Life satisfaction (round 2)		
(round 1)	r	R^2	b
Men			
Health self-rating	.30	.08	.26
Confidant	.08	.09	.36
Women			
Health self-rating	.20	.04	.20

Note.—Men = 206; women = 189.
* All predictors add a significant increase in variance at .05 level.
Source. Second longitudinal study.

Table 7-5. *Significant* predictors of affect balance (multiple regression).*

Predictor	Affect balance (round 2)		
(round 1)	r	R^2	b
Men			
Health self-rating	.24	.06	.57
Organizational activity	.10	.07	.13
Women			
Health self-rating	.35	.16	.87
Social leisure hours	.29	.22	.13
Sex enjoyment	.14	.25	.72

Note.—Men = 207; women = 189.
* All predictors add a significant increase in variance at .05 level.
Source. Second longitudinal study.

Consequences

As we have seen, considerable research has explored the antecedents of life satisfaction, but as far as we know no research has dealt with the possible consequences of life satisfaction among the aged. But since previous research has been cross-sectional, associations between life satisfaction and various factors could indicate that the factors were consequences of life satisfaction rather than vice versa (unless the factors clearly came first, such as sex, race, and education). It seems reasonable to hypothesize that greater life satisfaction could contribute to better health through better mental health, better motivation to take care of one's health, and through the prevention of various psychogenic illnesses which can result from anxiety, depression, and psychological stress. Similarly, greater life satisfaction could contribute to more social activity through better mental health, a positive attitude toward people, and through the prevention of isolation which can result from depression and pessimism.

Table 7-6. *Significant* predictors of anomie (multiple regression).*

Predictor	Anomie (round 2)		
(round 1)	r	R²	b
Men			
Verbal intelligence	−.47	.31	−.15
Internal control	−.17	.34	−.45
Age	.15	.37	.06
Education	−.49	.39	−.10
Social leisure hours	−.14	.42	−.06
Women			
Education	−.54	.26	−.21
Health self-rating	−.29	.31	−.24
Internal control	−.20	.35	−.42
Verbal intelligence	−.53	.37	−.10
Age	.21	.39	.04

Note.—Men = 201; women = 182.
* All predictors add a significant increase in variance at .05 level.
Source. Second longitudinal study.

Table 7-7. *Significant* consequences of life satisfaction indicators (correlation matrix).*

Life satisfaction indicator (round 1)	Consequences (round 2)				
	Health self-rating	Physical function	Total activity	Intimate contacts	Leisure activity
Men					
Life satisfaction	.20	.20	.44	–	—
Happiness attitudes	–	–	.30	–	–
Women					
Life satisfaction	.50	–	.60	.35	.42
Happiness attitudes	.38	–	.38	–	.35

Note.—Men = 92; women = 88.
* All consequences shown were significant at .05 level.
Source. First longitudinal study.

Because we have longitudinal data, we can examine which of these factors are predicted by life satisfaction and may therefore be a consequence. In the first study, we examined the correlations of round 1 life satisfaction and happiness attitudes with round 2 health self-rating, physical function, total activity, intimate contacts and leisure activity. Among both men and women the strongest correlations were with total activity, although women also had fairly strong correlations between life satisfaction and health self-rating, intimate contacts, and leisure activities (Table 7-7). These correlations are about the same magnitude as those in Table 7-1 which considers these same factors as antecedents of life satisfaction. This indicates that

Table 7-8. *Significant* consequences of life satisfaction indicators (correlation matrix).*

Life satisfaction indicator (round 1)	Consequences (round 2)			
	Health self-rating	Physical function	Organizational activity	Leisure social hours
Men				
Life satisfaction ladder	.26	–	.21	.16
Affect balance	.16	–	–	.17
Anomie	−.16	−.14	–	—
Women				
Life satisfaction ladder	.28	.18	.17	–
Affect balance	–	–	.19	.14
Anomie	−.14	–	–	−.21

Note.—Men = 226; women = 216.
* All consequences shown were significant at .05 level.
Source. Second longitudinal study.

health and activity are as likely to be consequences of life satisfaction as they are to be antecedent.

Similarly in the second longitudinal study, there are several significant correlations between round 1 indicators of life satisfaction and round 2 indicators of health and activity (Table 7-8). Here, too, the correlations are about the same magnitude as those in Table 7-3 which considers the factors as antecedents.

Thus, the evidence indicates that there is mutual interaction such that health and activity contribute to life satisfaction and life satisfaction in turn contributes to health and activity.

Additional evidence that life satisfaction can contribute toward health is the fact that in the first longitudinal study, longevity was significantly predicted by life satisfaction in the total group, by work satisfaction among men, and by the happiness rating among women (Table 4-10). This is true even after age and initial physical function status were controlled in the multiple regressions.

Summary

Many consider life satisfaction to be the ultimate criteria of "successful aging." It may also contribute to better health and a longer life. Previous studies are evenly split between those which found greater life satisfaction at later ages, less satisfaction at later ages, and no difference between ages. These contradictory findings may result from the different measures used: most studies with positive associations between age and life satisfaction have used global measures, while most with negative associations used measures of current happiness. Or the contradictions may result from the different periods surveyed: most of the earlier studies found negative associations, while the more recent ones found positive or no associations.

However, all the previous studies were cross-sectional and therefore were unable to determine whether the age differences represented true aging effects or cohort differences. The first longitudinal study found no evidence for any consistent increase or decrease in life satisfaction. The second study also found no consistent change in life satisfaction, except that there were significant increases in anomie among the women, especially during their late 50s and 60s. Similarly, there was no noticeable trend toward more homogeneity or heterogeneity in life satisfaction.

Previous studies have consistently found moderate to strong associations between life satisfaction and health, socioeconomic status, and social activity. Some studies have found associations between life satisfaction and continued employment, being married, and being white; but these associations tended to disappear when health and SES were controlled. There were no consistent nor substantial differences between men and women in life satisfaction.

However, since all the previous studies were cross-sectional they could not determine whether these correlates caused life satisfaction or vice versa. The analysis of antecedents and consequences of life satisfaction in the longitudinal studies indicates that health and social activity are probably both causes and effects of life satisfaction. Maintenance of financial status and sexual enjoyment were also strong predictors of life satisfaction. Lower socioeconomic status was a stronger predictor of anomie than of other measures of life satisfaction.

In summary, our evidence indicates that the most important ways to maintain life satisfaction in late life are maintaining health, financial status, social activity, and sexual activity.

Chapter 8. Conclusions

We have reviewed the previous studies and how our longitudinal findings confirm or modify existing theories in the areas of socioeconomic status, retirement, social activities, social networks, sexual behavior, and life satisfaction. We have done this largely because existing theories are based primarily on cross-sectional studies, which cannot distinguish between aging effects and cohort effects; and which cannot distinguish between causes, effects, and spurious associations. Our longitudinal data allowed us to measure aging effects separately from cohort differences, and to distinguish between predictor variables and consequent variables. By using multiple regression analysis we have identified spurious associations that are due to intercorrelations with third variables. We also used multiple regression analysis to estimate the relative importance of predictor and consequent variables when other variables are simultaneous controlled. Residual change analysis showed which variables predicted change in an outcome variable when its initial level was controlled.

What can we conclude from all these analyses, graphs, and statisticial tables? Each of the previous chapters includes a summary section which summarizes the major conclusions of that chapter, but it may be useful here to review these conclusions as they relate to the five major theoretical issues outlined in the first chapter: disengagement, activity, and continuity theories; age stratification; minority group therapy; life events and stress theory; and homogeneity *vs.* heterogeneity. The second part of this chapter discusses the implications of our conclusions.

Major Issues

Disengagement, Activity, and Continuity Theories

Recall that there are several issues involved in these theories. First, do most older people progressively disengage from social interaction as they grow older? Our longitudinal studies agree with most previous research that this is true for most older persons in most, but not all types of activity. The proportion retired clearly increases with age and the amount worked by those few who continue to work tends to decrease. Also total social activity tends to decline on the average at all age levels for both men and women. However, there is considerable variation within the groups at any one point in time and in the amount and direction of change over time. There are also substantial minorities who maintain or increase their social activity as they age. Furthermore, certain types of social activity do not seem to decline among our participants. For example, there seems to be no overall decline in club activities, and there is a tendency to increase church attendance through the 60s after which it levels off in the 70s and begins to decline in late old age. Also, despite shifts in the types of persons in the social networks (generally from older to younger), the total number of persons in the networks tends to remain constant. Thus, disengagement in the sense of total isolation was rare among our participants.

The majority of older persons did tend to disengage from sexual activity, partly because of widowhood and partly because of declining health. But here too, there is a substantial minority who maintain or even increase their sexual activity. Thus, while the first hypothesis of disengagement theory is generally true for the majority in most types of social activity, it is not true for substantial minorities and is not true in some types of activity.

The second issue involved is whether disengagement or activity contributes to better health, adjustment, and life satisfaction? Disengagement from employment (retirement) does not appear to have generally negative effects. There appears to be no increase in physical or mental illness, nor in mortality, caused by retirement. Nor does retirement generally tend to decrease life satisfaction: those few with decreases in life satisfaction tend to be balanced by those with increases. However, involuntary retirement tended to have negative effects on life satisfaction, while return to work tended to have positive effects. In general, the fact of retirement appears to be less important than one's attitude toward it and what one does in place of full-time employment.

As for social activity, our studies found clear evidence that various forms of activity tend to predict better health, happiness, and longevity. The strongest social activity predictors of health and happiness were more leisure activities, more secondary group activities, more people seen, and more hours in social activity. Greater longevity among men was predicted by more work satisfaction and secondary group activity, even after health and other factors were controlled.

As for social networks, disengagement from spouse (usually because of widowhood) tended to result in poorer health and less satisfaction among the middle-aged participants, but not among the older participants. Maintenance of sexual activity tends to predict better health and happiness among both men and women especially in the 50s and 60s, but does not appear related to longevity. Children leaving home does not usually produce long-term negative effects. In fact, the last child leaving home tended to increase life satisfaction and happiness. On the other hand, children living nearby predicted maintenance of life satisfaction among the women. Similarly, having more friends nearby predicted more happiness among the women. Furthermore, number of friends predicted better health among both men and women, although it has no significant relationship to longevity. Thus, the second hypothesis of disengagement theory is generally not true; activity, not disengagement tends to predict better life satisfaction, health, and longevity.

The third issue, which derives from continuity theory, is whether elders tend to maintain similar attitudes, levels of function, and activities relative to their age cohorts despite overall changes with age. Our longitudinal studies found much evidence to support continuity theory in this respect. The best single predictor of a person's status, attitude, or activity was usually their score on that same variable at a previous point in time. Persons who were wealthier, healthier, more employed, more active, and more satisfied at the beginning of our studies tended to be wealthier, more employed, more active, and more satisfied at the end of our studies, despite all the age changes that took place. Most individuals did, however, show some fluctuation in at least one round.

Age Stratification

A major problem here is the separation of age, period, and cohort effects. The lower socioeconomic status of older persons was found to be a mixture of aging and cohort effects. The lower education of elders is entirely due to cohort differences in that elders grew up in an era when there was less education in general. The lower occupations of elders is mainly a cohort effect, although some may have drifted down toward lower status occupation in old age. The lower income of elders is partly a cohort effect (due to their lower education and occupations) and partly an aging effect caused by retirement and/or disability. However, the longitudinal studies found less decline in adequacy of income than in amounts of income, and found no decline in feelings of status.

Retirement has been increasing among men but decreasing among women. This appears to be due to period effects such as increasing availability of retirement benefits for men and the increasing labor force participation of women. The result has been increasing age effects on the retirement of both men and women. In other words, age stratification in terms of employment has increased over time.

The general declines in total social activity are probably due primarily to aging effects. The increasing proportions of elders married and living with spouse appear to be due to the increasing health and longevity of later cohorts rather than general period effects. This cohort effect is even stronger among men than women because women's longevity has been increasing more rapidly than men's. Thus, age stratification by marital status has been decreasing over time.

There were little or no aging effects on life satisfaction or happiness among our longitudinal participants. Those with decreases tended to be balanced by those with increases. However, there may have been a period effect which has increased the life satisfaction of elders compared to younger persons.

Therefore, some cross-sectional differences between age groups (or age stratification) are primarily due to aging effects and some are primarily cohort effects and some are a mixture of the two effects. Some longitudinal changes are primarily due to aging effects and some are due to a mixture of aging and period effects. Longitudinal and cross-sequential analysis has helped separate these various effects.

Minority Group Theory

The main issue here is the usefulness of viewing the aged as a minority group in our society. Specifically, is there prejudice and discrimination against the aged which makes them suffer from lower status, economic deprivation, segregation, and loss of roles? In other words to what extent do they suffer from ageism?

Our studies and previous studies have shown that the usual prejudices against the aged are not true of most persons over 65. Most older persons are not sick or disabled. Only about one-fifth of persons over age 65 are so sick or disabled that they cannot engage in their normal activities. Most older persons are not senile in the sense of being seriously disoriented, demented, or having defective memories. Most participants in our studies tended to maintain good or adequate mental capacities until shortly before death. Most older persons are not in poverty. Only about one-seventh of persons over 65 have incomes below the official government poverty levels. Most persons in our studies tended to maintain good or adequate incomes throughout the study. Most older persons are not socially withdrawn or isolated. Despite some declines in total activities, most persons tended to maintain normal social activities among relatives, friends, and in churches and voluntary organizations. Most healthy married older persons are not sexually inactive. Despite declines in frequency, the majority of older couples remain sexually active at least into their 70s. Some even become more sexually active. Most older persons are not depressed or miserable. Most of our participants tended to maintain normal levels of happiness and life satisfaction throughout the studies, despite various declines and potentially stressful life events.

On the other hand, there were overall declines in employment, income, total social activity, and sexual activity. These declines were probably contributed to by such forms of age discrimination as age-related mandatory retirement, avoidance of older persons by younger persons, and discouragement of certain activities by family and friends.

The aged are of course different from the usual minority groups in that the aged are not born into their group and many aged often deny being "aged." However, the frequency of various forms of prejudice and discrimination against the aged makes minority group theory useful.

Life Events and Stress Theory

There are three issues involved in these theories: (1) Do major events in later life such as retirement, widowhood, illness, children leaving home, or moving, produce stress that results in physical and/or mental illness? (2) Do these events have additive or multiplicative effects so that persons with more such events are more likely to develop physical and mental illness? (3) Do physical, psychological, or social resources tend to improve adjustment to these events?

The event of retirement by itself does not usually produce enough stress to result in long-term negative adjustment. Retirement does not appear to increase overall morbidity or mortality, although sick people retire more than healthy people. It does not appear to cause an increase in mental illness, at least among those with moderate to high income and education. Retirement does not usually cause a decrease in life satisfaction, and those who are less satisfied after retirement tend to be balanced by those who are more satisfied. However, *mandatory* retirement tends to have negative effects on life satisfaction, adjustment, and activity; while return to work tended to have positive effects. When retirement is accompanied by sharp declines in adequacy of income or illness and disability, the result is often decreased life satisfaction; but this decrease may be more the result of the declines in income and health than the result of retirement as such. Spouse's retirement appears to have no significant negative effects.

The event of widowhood appears to be more stressful in middle age than in old age. Widowhood in middle age appears to produce lower morale, lower income, more institutionalization, and higher morbidity and mortality rates. However, widowhood in old age appeared to have no measurable long-term negative effects. In fact, death of spouse in late life appeared to bring relief and improved adjustment for many who had been suffering through the ordeal of their spouse's disability and terminal illness. Even among the middle-aged, the long-term effects of widowhood appeared to be relatively small.

Children leaving home do not usually produce long-term negative effects. In fact, the last child leaving home usually appears to increase happiness and life satisfaction.

Major medical events (those requiring hospitalization) produce the expected decline in health and some decline in activity, but produce no significant long-term decline in any other measures of adjustment.

Thus, there is little evidence that single life events are usually stressful enough to produce much long-term negative adjustment. However, there is evidence that the combination of several life events occuring close together is often stressful enough to produce negative outcomes. These effects appear to be additive so that the larger the number of events occurring, the larger the negative effects.

As for the effects of resources on adaptation to such events, psychological resources (such as intelligence and mental health) and social resources (such as higher socioeconomic status and larger social networks) help to maintain health, happiness, and life satisfaction, but do not affect other measures of social-psychological adjustment. Greater health resources appear to help in maintaining health after these events, but do not appear to help in social-psychological adaptation.

Homogeneity vs. Heterogeneity

The issue here is whether individuals become more like each other or more different from each other as they age. A specific form of this issue is whether men and women become more alike or different from each other in old age.

In terms of income we found that they tended to become more homogeneous as their real income tended to decline. They also probably become more homogeneous in terms of assets, as assets are used up by medical and other expenses typical of old age.

Retirement probably has a two-stage effect on homogeneity of activities and life style: during the early 60s when some are retiring but many are not, there is probably an increase in heterogeneity; but in the later 60s when most have retired homogeneity increases. In terms of differences between men and women, retirement clearly makes the men more like the majority of women (who had not been working full-time in middle-age).

In terms of social activities, previous research has reported conflicting results, while the Duke studies found little evidence for either increasing homogeneity or heterogeneity. Nor was there much evidence for greater or less similarity between men and women in social activities. Men's social networks became more similar to women's as they retired and became more dependent on family and friends for interaction. But widowhood tended to increase differences in social networks between men and women because it occurred to women more often than to men.

Like retirement, sexual activity probably also goes thorough two stages in terms of homogeneity. Heterogenity tends to increase during their 60s as some decrease their sexual activity and others do not; but in their 70s and 80s homogeneity increases as sexual activity declines to the vanishing point. Similarly, the differences between men and women tend to increase during their 60s and then decline as most of both sexes become sexually inactive.

Finally, there was little evidence for any trend toward homogeneity or heterogeneity in life satisfaction, nor in such differences between men and women.

Thus, older people tend to become first more heterogeneous during their 50s and early 60s in terms of employment and sexual activity; and then become more homogeneous as these variables decline. Income homogeneity increases as real income declines. However, there appear to be no clear trends in terms of social activities or life satisfaction.

Longitudinal vs. *Cross-Sectional Studies*

Rather than a theoretical issue, this is a methodological issue with many implications for theories of aging. The issue is whether longitudinal or cross-sequential studies are worth their greater costs per participant (since each participant must be interviewed several times) and longer time-span (since interviews must be repeated over a period of years). In order to evaluate this issue we will briefly review the major types of findings which were possible *only* with a longitudinal or cross-sequential design. Many of these findings have already been reviewed in relation to the major issues, but here the emphasis is on the longitudinal or cross-sequential analysis that produced the findings.

The cross-sequential analysis of socioeconomic status showed that educational differences between age groups are primarily a cohort effect; that occupational differences are also primarily cohort effects, although aging accounts for some of the differences (through increasing disabilities and partial retirement); and that income differences are also a mixture of cohort and aging effects. It also showed that adequacy of income was perceived to decline less than actual income declined. Also feelings of status did not decline over time. Longitudinal analysis showed that there was considerable continuity in income, because despite general income declines, prior income was the best single predictor of later income. It also showed a general trend toward more homogeneity in income in the later years. Longitudinal analysis showed that consequences of higher socioeconomic status were the maintenance of better health, higher cognitive function, and more life satisfaction over time.

A cross-sequential analysis of retirement found that there were strong aging effects among both men and women and that these effects have been increasing over time (a period effect). Retirement causes declines in income, productive hours, active hours, and some social activities; but has little or no effect on health, longevity, happiness, or life satisfaction except when it is mandatory or accompanied by illness and disability.

Although total social activities decline with age on the average, longitudinal analysis found considerable variability between and within groups in the amount and direction of change with age. There were substantial minorities who maintain or increase their social activity. There also was little or no change with age in organizational participation. There was strong continuity in rank ordering of participants in social activity, but no clear evidence for increasing homogeneity or heterogeneity. Predictors of social activity varied by type of activity. Various forms of social activity were found predictive of better health, longevity, happiness, and life satisfaction.

Cross-sequential analysis of marital status found in addition to the expected aging effect, a cohort effect which increased the proportions in a given age group who remained married and living with spouse. A contrasting period effect increased the proportion living alone. Longitudinal analysis showed a shift from older persons in the social network to younger persons, but a fairly constant total number of persons. Widowhood produced more negative effects in middle age than old age, but children leaving home usually had no negative effects in either age group.

Longitudinal analysis found that despite average declines in sexual activity substantial minorities maintain or even increase sexual activity at least through their 70s. Previous sexual activity and pleasure were the best predictors of later sexual activity. Sexual activity appears to contribute to health, happiness, and life satisfaction.

Lastly, longitudinal analysis found little or no change in life satisfaction as persons grew older. The analysis of antecedents and consequences of life satisfaction found evidence that life satisfaction may contribute to health and social activity as well as vice versa.

Thus, most of the findings reported in this monograph are evidence of the value of longitudinal and cross-sequential analysis. Cross-sectional studies are also valuable and are less expensive and time consuming, but there are many questions about aging that can only be answered by longitudinal studies.

Implications

If you have read this far you may have wondered, "So what?" What practical or policy implications could be drawn from this research? I believe that the primary role of the scientist is to discover and present facts, rather than to render value judgments as to right and wrong or what "ought to be done. I believe that the value judgments of scientists should be given no more weight than those of any other intelligent and well-informed citizen. Nevertheless, it may be useful to present my opinions as to the major practical and policy implications of this research.

Prejudice

I hope these findings will be used to reduce the prejudices and unwarranted fears about aging that are so widespread in our society. It should be clear that most elders do not fit any simple stereotype about the aged, neither the negative nor positive stereotypes. In most respects the aged are at least as heterogeneous as any other age group; and while there may be increasing homogeneity in some respects in some age ranges, there is increasing heterogeneity in other respects and in other age ranges. Furthermore, declines in functioning are neither universal, inevitable, nor constant. The dominant pattern is one of continuity so that older persons tend to remain pretty much the kinds of people they were when younger. Yet within this dominant pattern there are considerable fluctuations, both declines and improvements, some temporary, some permanent.

More specifically, most elders are not sick nor disabled, despite widespread beliefs to the contrary. On the contrary, most elders are able to engage in their normal activities and lead normally healthy lives. Similarly, most elders are not senile in any clinical sense, but rather are able to carry out normal cognitive functions. Most elders are not in poverty, despite declines in income. Most elders are not isolated, but rather maintain normal social relations, substituting relations with younger persons as relations with older persons drop out. Nor are they miserable and depressed.

In sum, the average person need not fear illness, disability, senility, poverty, isolation, nor depression in old age because the odds are that these things will not happen to him or her.

Discrimination

I hope these findings will be used to reduce the many overt and covert forms of discrimination against the aged in our society. Specifically, I think mandatory retirement because of age alone, regardless of which age is chosen, should usually be prohibited. There may be some exceptions to this general rule when there are "*bona fide* age qualifications" or when objectively determining individual ability is impractical. I believe this mainly because mandatory retirement based on age is contrary to our democratic principles of judging each individual on his or her own merit and abilities; and also because our and other's studies have shown that many individuals forced to retire are still capable of performing their jobs efficiently and effectively, and that mandatory retirement often has detrimental effects on the individual.

Because our study and other studies have shown the value of education, adequate income, active leisure, and group participation, I think the subtle discriminations which reduce these things for elders should be eliminated. Furthermore, I think private and public programs should be expanded to increase elders opportunities for more education, income, active leisure, and group participation.

Health Maintenance

Because our studies have shown health to be such an important factor in successful aging, I believe many things could and should be done to improve the health of elders. Since "an ounce of prevention is worth a pound of cure," primary emphasis should be placed on improving the hygiene and healthy habits of both elders and those approaching old age. This includes such well-known but critical practices as a nutritious but moderate diet to avoid obesity, daily exercise to keep the body and especially the cardiovascular system fit, avoiding cigarettes, avoiding excessing drinking, and medical check-ups whenever there are symptoms. Medicare and Medicaid should be improved to reduce the many financial barriers to adequate medical care. Training in geriatrics should become a regular part of every medical student's curriculum, rather than being ignored as in most medical schools today. Practicing physicians should also get training in geriatrics to improve their care of elders. Perhaps as important as formal training in geriatrics is a modification of health professionals' attitudes so that they do not regard illness and disability among the aged as "normal" nor assume that "nothing can be done" about illnesses associated with old age.

Plan for Retirement

The individuals approaching retirement can do much to prepare for and improve adjustment to old age. First, they can take care of their health as described above. They should also make certain that they have adequate medical insurance or can afford the medical care they may need. They cannot count on Medicare to cover the majority of their medical expenses. Second, they can plan for some part-time employment or other useful activity to take the place of their regular employment. They can plan and develop skills and interests in hobbies and group activities to keep them active, interested, and interesting. Our research has shown this to be an important factor in maintaining health and happiness. Third, they can prepare to maintain the adequacy of their income through part-time employment, savings, and investments. Fourth, they can explore the many options retired persons have as to where and how they want to live. After they have decided which option is most attractive to them, they can prepare to make that option a reality upon retirement, rather than an impractical dream.

More Research

It should be obvious that much more research is needed to explore the remaining mysteries of aging and to improve the quality and quantity of late life. Gerontology is a relatively young science and our research raises as many questions as it answers. Perhaps one of the most important implications of our research is that longitudinal and cross-sequential studies, with their unique ability to study aging processes over time, as well as their antecedents and consequences, can make a vital contribution to the growing science of gerontology. And gerontology is, after all, the science of that culmination stage of life to which we all aspire.

Appendix. Variables in the Longitudinal Studies

(All values are for round 1)

Achievement values (second longitudinal study). Based on the number of the following statements with which the participant disagreed: "In his work, all a person should want is a secure, not too difficult job, with enough pay for a nice car and home of his own. When a person is born the success he is going to have is already in the cards, so he may as well accept it and not fight against it. The secret of happiness is not expecting too much out of life and being content with what comes your way. Nothing is worth the sacrifice of moving away from one's parents. It is best to have a job as part of an organization all working together, even if you don't get individual credit. Planning only makes a person unhappy since your plans hardly ever work out anyway. Nowadays with world conditions the way they are, the wise person lives for today and lets tomorrow take care of itself."

Scores could range from 0 to 7 with higher scores representing higher achievement values. Mean for men = 4.7, *SD* = 1.6; mean for women = 4.6, *SD* = 1.4

Active hours (second longitudinal study). Based on the number of hours per week reported in the following activities: playing a sport or working on a hobby; going to a sports event such as a baseball or football game; attending church or other meetings (including lectures, plays, concerts), doing volunteer work for church, other organizations, or relatives; visiting, telephoning, or writing friends or relatives, parties, eating out, or entertaining; yard care, gardening, repairing, building, mending, sewing, other such activities. Mean = 64.0, *SD* = 170.

Affect balance (second longitudinal study). Based on the Bradburn and Caplovitz scale, which consisted of four negative emotions (very lonely or remote from other people; depressed or very unhappy; bored; so restless you couldn't sit long in a chair) and four positive emotions (on top of the world; particularly excited or interested in something; pleased about having accomplished something; proud because someone complimented you on something you had done).

Responses were scored as 0 for "not at all"; 1 for "once"; 2 for "several times"; and 3 for "often." The sum of the scores on the responses to the negative items were subtracted from the sum of the scores on the responses to the positive items for the affect balance score. Mean = 1.1; *SD* = 2.8.

Anomie scale (second longitudinal study). Based on the agree-disagree responses to the following nine statements: "With everything so uncertain these days, it almost seems as though anything could happen. What is lacking in the world today is the old kind of friendship that lasted for a lifetime. With everything in such a state of disorder, it's hard for a person to know where he stands from one day to the next. Everything changes so quickly these days that I often have trouble deciding which are the right rules to follow. I often feel that many things our parents stood for are just going to ruin before our very eyes. The trouble with the world today is that most people don't really believe in anything. I often feel awkward and out of place. People were better off in the old days when everyone knew just how he was expected to act. It seems to me that other people find it easier to decide what is right than I do."

One point was given for each statement agreed with, so scores could range from 0 to 9. Mean for men = 4.2, *SD* = 2.3; mean for women = 3.8, *SD* = 2.2.

Busy (second longitudinal study). Based on responses to one of the Semantic Differential items with the bipolar adjectives "Busy-Inactive." The respondent checked a point along a 7-point scale representing "What I really am." Seven represented very busy and one represented very inactive. Mean for men = 5.7, *SD* = 1.1; mean for women = 6.0, *SD* 1.0.

Change in financial status (first longitudinal study). Based on responses to the question, "Are you in a better or a worse financial position than you were at age 55?" Responses were coded 1 for "worse now"; 2 for "about the same"; and 3 for "better now." Mean for men = 2.1, *SD* = 0.9; mean for women = 2.1, *SD* = 0.9.

Children nearby (second longitudinal study). Based on responses to the question, "Do any of your children live outside your household but within an hour's travel? If so, how many?" Mean for men = 1.0, *SD* = 1.3; mean for women = 0.7, *SD* = 1.0.

Church meetings (second longitudinal study). Based on responses to the question, "How many times a month do you attend religious services?" Nine was the maximum number of times coded. Mean for men = 3.8, *SD* = 2.3; mean for women = 2.2, *SD* = 2.2.

Class identification (second longitudinal study). Based on responses to the question, "Which of the following descriptions best fits you?" Responses were coded 1 for "upper class"; 2 "upper middle class"; 3 for "middle class"; 4 for "working class"; and 5 for "lower class." Mean for men = 3.1, *SD* = 0.8; mean for women = 2.9, *SD* = 0.8.

Close friends (second longitudinal study). Based on "Do you have any close friends (other than relatives) living within an hour's travel? (Persons you could ask to do a real favor.)" If yes, "How many?" (more than 9 was coded as 9). Mean for men = 6.6, *SD* = 3.0; mean for women = 5.5, *SD* = 2.9.

Confidant (second longitudinal study). Based on responses to the question, "Is there one person in particular you talk to or confide in about your problems?" "No" was coded 0 and "Yes" was coded 1. Sixty percent said "yes".

Contacts with children (second longitudinal study). Based on responses to the question, "About how many times a month do you visit with or telephone your children?" Mean = 13.1.

Contact with children and young friends (first longitudinal study). Based on responses to the question, "Do you often see or hear from children or young people who are friends? (Include nieces, nephews or grandchildren if 20 years old or younger.)" Responses were coded 0 for "has none"; 1 for "less than once a year"; 2 "for a few times a year"; 12 for "once or twice a month"; 50 for "about once a week"; and 365 for "everyday." Mean for men = 143, SD = 160, mean for women = 164, SD = 169.

Contact with friends (first longitudinal study). Based on responses to the question, "Do you see your friends more or less often now than when you were 55 years old?" Responses were coded 1 for "less often now"; 2 for "about the same"; and 3 for "more often now." Mean for men = 1.6, SD = 0.8; mean for women = 1.8, SD = 0.8.

Contact with relatives (first longitudinal study). Based on responses to the question, "How often do you see some of your family or close relatives?" Responses were coded 0 for "has none"; 1 for "less than once a year"; 2 for "once a year or more, but less than once a month"; 12 for "about once a month"; 50 for "once or twice a week"; and 365 for "every day." Mean for men = 347, SD = 78; mean for women = 277, SD = 152.

Contact with relatives (second longitudinal study). Based on responses to the question, "About how many times a month do you visit with or telephone them (close relatives)?" Mean = 14.0.

Current financial status (first longitudinal study). Based on responses to question, "How would you describe your present financial position in life?" Responses were coded 1 for "can't make ends meet"; 2 for "enough to get along"; and 3 for "comfortable, well-to-do, or wealthy." Mean for men = 2.4, SD = 0.7; mean for women = 2.4, SD = 0.6.

Employment (first longitudinal study). Present work status was coded as 1 for not working; 2 for part-time work; 3 for full-time work.

Feeling useful (second longitudinal study). Based on an item from the Semantic Differential Scale with the two polar adjectives "useless" and "useful" and a scale from 1 to 7 on which respondents put a check to indicate "What I really am." Mean = 5.5; SD = 1.0.

Free time (second longitudinal study). Based on responses to the question, "Are you satisfied with the amount of free time you have now, or do you feel you have too much free time or too little free time?" Responses were: "I am satisfied with the amount of free time I now have" (68 percent); "I have too much free time" (6%); "I have too little free time" (25 percent).

Friends among neighbors (second longitudinal study). Based on responses to the question, "How many of your neighbors (other than close friends and relatives) do you know well enough to visit in their home?" Responses were coded 0 to 9 with 9 for 9 or more. Mean for men = 5.3, SD = 2.8; mean for women = 4.5, SD = 2.8.

Happiness attitude (first longitudinal study). Based on responses to the six statements in the Happiness subscale of the Chicago Inventory of Activities and Attitudes (Cavan et al., 1949). The possible responses were "agree, disagree, or uncertain." One point was added for agreement with each of 3 positive statements: "I am just as happy as when I was younger. These are the best years of my life. My life is so enjoyable that I almost wish it would go on forever." One point was subtracted for agreement with each of 3 negative statements: "This is the saddest time of my life. I seem to have less and less reason to live. My life is full of worry." Three points were added to the results so that the scores could range from 0 to 6. Mean for men = 4.4, SD = 1.2; mean for women = 4.2, SD = 1.6.

Happiness rating (first longitudinal study). This was a rating of the participant's overall happiness by the interviewing social worker based on the responses to the social history interview. The rating could range from 0 for "unhappy or discontented, worried, fearful, frustrated" to 9 for "very happy, exultant, great contentment." Mean for men = 3.4, SD = 1.6; mean for women = 3.8, SD = 1.6.

Health self-rating (first longitudinal study). Based on responses to the question, "How would you rate your health at the present time?" Responses were coded as 1 for "very poor or poor"; 2 for "fair or fair for my age"; 3 for "good or good for my age"; and 4 for "excellent or excellent for my age." Mean for men = 2.8, SD = 0.9; mean for women = 2.8, SD = 1.0.

Hours worked (second longitudinal study). Based on the question, "How many hours a day do you usually spend working (or housework) including travel to work?" The response was multiplied by the number of days worked per week. Mean = 34.

Household (second longitudinal study). Based on responses to the question, "How many people live with you in your household?" Mean for men = 1.4, SD = 0.8; mean for women = 1.3, SD = 1.0.

Income (second longitudinal study). Based on responses to the question, "About how much was your (and your spouse's) total income from all sources during the past 12 months?" Responses were coded into $1,000 intervals up to $7,000; $7,000 to $9,000; $15,000 and over. Mean = $9,300.

Intercourse frequency (first longitudinal study). Based on responses to an item in the medical history titled, "Present frequency of intercourse." Responses were coded 0 for "none"; 1 for "once a month or less"; 2 for "once every two weeks (include every 3 weeks)"; 4 for "once every week"; 8 for "more than once a week";

and 4 for "active, frequency unspecified." Mean for married men = 1.4, *SD* = 2.0; mean for married women = 1.2, *SD* = 21.

Internal control (second longitudinal study). Based on choices of the "internal" (I) statement as being more true than the "external" (E) statement in each of the following 4 pairs of statements: (*a*) some of the good and some of the bad things in my life have happened by chance (E), (*b*) what's happened to me has been my own doing (I); (*a*) when I make plans, I am almost certain that I can make them work (I), (*b*) I have usually found that what is going to happen will happen regardless of my plans (E); (*a*) I like to do things on the spur of the moment (E), (*b*) I prefer to have things all planned out in advance (I); (*a*) I often seem to have little influence over what other people believe (E), (b) When I'm right, I can usually convince others (I)." Since there were four pairs of statements, scores could range from 0 to 4. Mean for men = 2.6, *SD* = 1.0; mean for women = 2.2, *SD* = 1.0.

Intimate contacts (first longitudinal study). Based on responses to five questions in the Chicago Inventory of Activities and Attitudes (Cavan et al., 1949) dealing with the person's household, how often the family is seen, whether the family neglects the person, how often the person sees friends, and how often the person sees children or younger persons. Scores could range from 0 to 10 with higher scores indicating more intimate contacts. Mean for men = 7.4, *SD* = 1.2; mean for women = 6.1, *SD* = 1.9.

Leisure activity (first longitudinal study). Based on responses to four questions in the Chicago Inventory of Activities and Attitudes (Cavan et al., 1949) dealing with the person's number of leisure activities listed, time spent in reading, number of organizations belongd to, and number of club meeting attended per month. Scores could range from 0 to 8 with high scores indicating more leisure activity. Mean for men = 4.6, *SD* = 2.1; mean for women = 5.6, *SD* = 2.2.

Life satisfaction (first longitudinal study). Based on responses to the attitudes items in the "Chicago Inventory of Activities and Attitudes" (Cavan et al., 1949). This scale consists of 56 agree-disagree items about the subject's satisfaction with 8 areas of life: health friends, work, economic security, religion, usefulness, family, and general happiness. The scale could range from 0 to 48 and higher scores indicate greater life satisfaction. Mean for men = 34.2, *SD* = 6.2; mean for women = 34.4, *SD* = 5.7.

Life satisfaction (second longitudinal study). Based on the "Cantril Ladder" technique of asking participants to place themselves on a ten-rung ladder with the bottom (0) representing "the worst possible life for you" and the top (9) representing "the best possible life for you." Mean = 7.0; *SD* = 1.4.

Longevity Difference (first longitudinal study). This is the difference between the number of years actually survived after the first examination, minus the number of years expected to survive based on age, sex, and race life expectancy tables for North Carolina. Positive values thus represent greater than expected longevity and negative values represent less than expected longevity. Mean = 0.1; *SD* = 5.5.

Medications Taken (second longitudinal study). Based on the question, "Below are a list of the medications that people often have to take or use. Circle any that you are taking now." Fifteen types of medications were listed along with a residual category, "other kinds of medicine." The number of medications circled was summed. Mean = 0.8; *SD* = 1.1.

Meeting hours (second longitudinal study). The number of hours per week reported spent "attending church or other meetings (including lectures, plays, concerts)." Mean for men = 2.3, *SD* = 1.7; mean for women = 2.9, *SD* = 2.6.

Meetings (first longitudinal study). Based on the question, "How often do you attend other meetings (nonreligious" Responses were coded 0 for "never"; 1 for "less than once a month"; 2 for "one to three times a month"; 3 for "once a week"; and 4 for "twice a week or more." Mean = 2.8.

Mental function (first longitudinal study). Based on the full scale weighted score on the Wechsler Adult Intelligence Scale (Wechsler, 1955). This scale consists of equally weighted scores on the 11 subscales: information, comprehension, arithmetic, similarities, digit span, vocabulary, digit symbol, picture completion, block design, picture arrangement, and object assembly. Mean = 81.7, *SD* = 33.1.

Mental function (second longitudinal study). The equally weighted sum of 4 subscales from the Wechsler Adult Intelligence Scale (Wechsler, 1955): Information, vocabulary, digit symbol, and picture arrangement. Mean for men = 35.8, *SD* = 9.7; mean for women = 36.9, *SD* = 8.8.

Musculoskeletal system rating (second longitudinal study). A 10-point rating scale by the examining physician ranging from 0 for "no evidence of musculoskeletal disease" to 9 for "severe arthritic deformity with total restriction of joint movements in all extremities, or cardiovascular attack with residual global paralysis of both sets of extremities." Mean = 0.5, *SD* = 0.9.

Nonchurch meetings (second longitudinal study). Based on responses to the question, "How many times a month do you attend meetings of other (nonchurch) groups such as clubs, unions, or associations?" Nine was the maximum number of meetings coded. Mean for men = 1.6, *SD* = 2.3; mean for women = 2.0, *SD* = 2.3.

Occupation (both studies). Primary occupations were dichotomized into manual (including craftsmen, foremen, operatives, semiskilled workers, service workers, unskilled laboreres, and farm laborers) and nonmanual (including professionals, managers and proprietors, farm managers or proprietors, clerical, sales, and technicians).

Old age identification (second longitudinal study). Based on responses to the question, "Which of these five terms describes you best? Young, middle aged, elderly, aged, old." "Young" and "middle aged" were coded 1. Mean for men = 0.3, SD = 0.5; mean for women = 0.3, SD = 0.4.

Organizational activity (second longitudinal study). The sum of number of religious services and number of meetings attended (see church meetings and nonchurch meetings). Mean for males = 5.3; SD = 3.9; mean for women = 5.8; SD = 4.0.

Performance intelligence (second longitudinal study). Based on the Digit Symbol and Picture Arrangement subscales of the Wechsler Adult Intelligence Scale (Wechsler, 1955). The scores were scaled to give each equal weight and the results summed. Mean for men = 14.3, SD = 4.4; mean for women = 15.6, SD = 4.4.

Persons seen (second longitudinal study). Based on the question, "Some people talk to a lot of people each day. Others do not. Look at these circles and imagine the center (1) stands for very few people. The largest circle (9) stands for very many people. Which circle describes how many people you talk to on an average day?" Mean = 5.5, SD = 3.9.

Physical function rating (first longitudinal study). A rating by the examining physician on a 6-point scale from 1 for limitation of over 80 percent to 6 for no pathology or limitation. Mean for men = 4.2, SD = 1.3; mean for women = 4.4, SD = 1.2.

Physical function rating (second longitudinal study). A rating by the examining physician on 10-point scale from 0 for "moribund" to 9 for "normal, no complaints, no evidence of disease." Mean for men = 8.2, SD = 0.8; mean for women = 8.3, SD = 0.7.

Pleasure in sex relations when younger (second longitudinal study). Based on responses to the question, "How much enjoyment and pleasure did you have during sex relations when you were younger?" Responses were coded 0 for "none"; 1 for "mild pleasure and enjoyment"; 2 for "moderate pleasure and enjoyment"; and 3 for "very much pleasure and enjoyment." Mean for married men = 2.6, SD = 0.6; mean for married women = 2.1, SD = 0.7.

Primary group activities (first longitudinal study). Based on the ratings given by the interviewing social worker of the amount of primary group (family and friends) activity. The ratings ranged from 0 for "alone in world—no family, relatives, or friends" to 9 for "daily contacts, group of long standing, closely incorporated into group life, important in determining group actions." Mean for men = 7.5, SD = 2.0; mean for women = 6.6, SD = 2.6.

Productive Hours (second longitudinal study). Based on the number of hours per week reported in the following activities: working (or housework) including travel to work; doing volunteer work for church, other organizations, or relatives; yard care, gardening, repairing, building, mending, sewing, and other such activities. Mean = 39.6.

Psychosomatic symptoms (second longitudinal study). Based on the question, "How often last week did you have: dizziness, general aches and pains, headaches, muscles twitches or trembling, nervousness or tenseness, rapid heart beat, sleeplessness, loss of appetite, constipation?" Responses were scored 0 for "not at all"; 1 for "once"; 2 for "several times"; and 3 for "nearly all the time." Scored responses were summed for total psychosomatic symptoms score. Mean = 3.7; SD = 3.8.

Race (first longitudinal study). Coded as 1 for whites and 2 for blacks.

Relatives nearby (second longitudinal study). Based on responses to the question, "Do you have any other close relatives (parents, brothers, sisters, uncles, aunts, nieces, nephews, and first cousins) living within an hour's travel from your home? If so, how many?" Mean for men = 3.8, SD = 3.7; mean for women = 4.0, SD = 3.6.

Religious services (first longitudinal study). Based on the question, "How often do you attend religious service?" Responses were coded 0 for "never"; 1 for "less than once a month"; 2 for "one to three times a month"; 3 for "once a week"; and 4 for "twice a week or more." Mean = 2.7.

Religious activities (first longitudinal study). Based on responses to three questions from the Chicago Inventory of Activities and Attitudes (Cavan et al., 1949). "How often do you attend religious services? Do you read religious literature?" The sum of responses could range from 0 for "never" responses to all three questions to 10 for attending religious services twice a week or more, listening to church services over the radio or TV 3 or more times weekly, and reading religious literature daily. Mean for men = 6.4, SD = 2.1; mean for women = 6.8, SD = 1.8.

Respected (second longitudinal study). Based on responses to one of the Semantic Differential items with the bipolar adjectives "respected–not respected." Respondents check a point along a 7-point scale representing "what I really am." Seven represented very respected and 1 represented very not respected. Mean for men = 6.7, SD = 0.7; mean for women = 6.8, SD = 0.5.

Secondary group contacts (first longitudinal study). Based on the ratings given by the interviewing social worker of the amount of secondary group (church, clubs, reading, TV) contacts. The rating ranged from 0 for "in no groups no reading, no radio, complete social isolation" to 9 for "time filled with many groups, much reading, many radio programs, always on the go or occupied with reading, TV, etc." Mean for men = 4.3, SD = 1.6; mean for women = 4.9, SD = 1.9.

Sedentary leisure hours (second longitudinal study). Based on the number of hours per week reported in the following activities: eating; watching TV or listening to the radio; reading newspapers, magazines, or books; just sitting around doing nothing, taking it easy. Mean = 33.5.

Sexual activity (first longitudinal study). Based on responses to an item in the medical history titled, "Present Frequency of Intercourse." Persons reporting "none" were classified as sexually inactive and persons reporting any intercourse were classified as active.

Sexual activity (second longitudinal study). Based on responses to the question, "How often, on the average, do you have sex relations at the present time?" Those who reported "never" were classified as sexually inactive and those who reported any sex relations were classified as active.

Sexual enjoyment (second longitudinal study). Based on responses to the question, "How much pleasure or enjoyment do you have during sex relations at the present time?" Responses were coded 0 for "none"; 1 for "mild pleasure and enjoyment"; 2 for "moderate pleasure and enjoyment"; and 3 for "very much pleasure and enjoyment." Mean for men = 1.9, SD = 1.0; mean for women = 0.9, SD = 1.0.

Sex relations frequency (second longitudinal study). Based on responses to the question, "How often, on the average, do you have sex relations at the present time?" Responses were coded 0 for "never"; 1 for "once a month or less frequently"; 4 for "once a week"; 12 for "three times a week"; and 15 for "more than 3 times a week." Mean for married men = 3.7, SD = 3.9; mean for married women = 2.0, SD = 3.7.

Sex relations frequency when younger (second longitudinal study). Based on responses to the question, "How often, on the average did you have sex relations when you were younger?" Responses were coded as 0 for "never"; 1 for "once a month or less frequently"; 4 for "once a week"; 12 for 3 times a week"; and 15 for "more than 3 times a week." Mean for married men = 11.0, SD = 10.0; mean for women = 8.0, SD = 7.0.

Social leisure hours (second longitudinal study). Based on the number of hours per week reported for the following activities: going to a sports event; attending church or other meetings; doing volunteer work for church, other organizations, or relatives; visiting, telephoning, or writing friends or relative, parties, eating out, or entertaining. Mean = 9.8; SD = 6.0.

Solitary hours (second longitudinal study). Based on the number of hours per week reported in the following activities: dressing, bathing, and personal care; watching TV or listening to the radio; reading; yard care, gardening, repairing, building, mending, sewing, and other such activities; just sitting around doing nothing. Mean = 34.0.

Symptoms checked (second longitudinal study). Based on the question, "Show by checking the following which are giving you trouble now or apply to you at the present time." Thirty common symptoms were listed for checking. Mean = 2.2; SD = 2.0.

Total activity (first longitudinal study). Based on responses to 20 questions dealing with 5 areas of activities: health (physical capacity to be active); family and friends (frequency of contact); leisure (ways of spending time, hobbies, reading, organizations); economic (amount of work or housework and lack of economic restrictions on activity); and religious activity (attendance at religious services, listening to them on radio or TV, reading religious literature) (Cavan et al., 1949). Each subscore could range from 0 to 10 with the higher scores indicating more activity. The total activity score is the sum of the subscore in these five areas (total range: 0 to 50). Mean for men = 27.2, SD = 6.2; mean for women = 30.1, SD = 5.8.

Total number in social network (second longitudinal study). The sum of the numbers in household, children outside household, relatives, friends, and neighbors. Mean for men = 18.1, SD = 6.5; mean for women = .612, SD = 6.1.

Verbal intelligence (second longitudinal study). Based on the information and vocabulary subscales of the Wechsler Adult Intelligence Scale (Wechsler, 1955). The scores were scaled to give each equal weight and the results summed. Mean for men = 21.5, SD = 6.1; mean for women = 21.3, SD = 5.5.

Visiting hours (second longitudinal study). The number of hours per week which were reported as spent "visiting, telephoning, or writing friends or relatives, parties, eating out, or entertaining." Mean for men = 4.9, SD = 3.6; mean for women = 7.1, SD = 6.7.

Weeks sick in bed (second longitudinal study). Based on the question, "During the past 12 months, how many days were you in bed all or most of the day because of illness or health conditions?" Responses were coded into approximate number of weeks. Mean = 0.65, SD = 1.5.

Work satisfaction (first longitudinal study). Based on a subscale of the Chicago Inventory of Activities and Attitudes (Cavan et al., 1949). One point was added for agreement with each of the following: "I am happy only when I have definite work to do. I am satisfied with the work I now do. I do better work now than ever before." One point was subtracted for disagreement with each of the following statements: "I can no longer do any kind of useful work. I have no work to look forward to. I get badly flustered when I have to hurry with my work." Three points were added all scores so that the range was from 0 to 6. Mean for men = 3.4, SD = 1.3; mean for women = 3.7, SD = 1.1

Bibliography

Administration on Aging, 1978. *Statistical Notes*. No. 2 (August).

Andrews, F., & Withey, S., 1976, *Social indicators of well-being*. New York: Plenum.

Atchley, R., 1976, Selected social and psychological differences between men and women in later life. *Journal of Gerontology*, 31:204-211.

Athcley, R., 1977. *Social forces in later life*. Belmont, Calif,: Wadsworth.

Babchuk, N., & Booth A., 1969. Voluntary association membership. *American Sociological Review* 34:31-45.

Babchuk, N., Peters, G., Horr, D., & Kaiser, M., 1979. The voluntary associations of the aged. *Journal of Gerontology*, 34:579-587.

Barfield, R., & Morgan, J., 1969. *Early retirement*. Ann Arbor: Institute for Social Research, University of Michigan.

Bartko, J., Patterson, R., & Butler, R., 1971. Biomedical and behavioral predictors of survival among normal aged men. In E. Palmore and F. Jeffers (Eds.), *Prediction of life span*. Lexington, Mass.: Heath Lexington Books.

Bell, R., 1971. *Marriage and family interaction*, 3rd Edition. Homewood, Ill.: Dorsey Press.

Berardo, F., 1968. Widowhood status in the U.S. *The Family Coordinator*, 17:191-203.

Berardo, F., 1970. Survivorship and social isolation. *The Family Coordinator*, 19:11-15.

Binstock, R., & Shanas, E. (Eds.), 1976. *Handbook of aging and the social sciences*. New York: Van Nostrand Reinhold.

Blau, Z., 1973. *Old age in a changing society*. New York: Watts.

Botwinick, J., 1977. Intellectual abilities. In J. Birven and K. Schaie (Eds.). *Handbook of the Psychology of Aging*. New York: Van Nostrand Reinhold.

Bradburn, N., 1969. *The structure of psychological well-being*. Chicago: Aldine.

Bradburn, N., & Caplovitz, D., 1965. *Reports on happiness*. Chicago: Aldine.

Bromley, D., 1966. *The psychology of human aging*, Baltimore: Penguin Books.

Bull, C., & Aucoin, J., 1975. Voluntary association participation and life satisfaction. *Journal of Gerontology*, 30:73-76.

Burgess, E., 1954. Social relations, activities, and personal adjustment. *American Journal of Sociology*, 59:352-360.

Cameron, P., 1968. Masculinity-feminity in the aged. *Journal of Gerontology*, 10:63-65

Campbell, A., Converse, P., & Rodgers, W., 1976. *The quality of American life*. New York: Russell Sage Foundation.

Cantril, H., 1965. *The pattern of human concern*. New Brunswick, N.J.: Rutgers University Press.

Carp, F., 8:184-88. 1968. Person-situation congruence in engagement. *Gerontologist*. 8:184-88.

Cavan, R., Burgess, E., Havighurst, R., & Goldhamer, H., 1949. *Personal adjustment in old age*. Chicago: Science Research Associate.

Center for the Study of Aging and Human Development, 1978. *Multidimensional functional assessment: The Oars methodology*. Durham, N.C.: Duke University.

Clark, M., & Anderson, B., 1967. *Culture and aging*. Springfield, Ill.: C. C. Thomas.

Cottrell, F., & Atchley, R., 1969. *Women in retirement*. Oxford, Ohio: Scripps Foundation.

Cronback, L., & Furby, L., 1970. How should we measure "change," or should we? *Psychology Bulletin*, 74:68-80.

Cumming, E., & Henry, W., 1961. *Growing old*. New York: Basic Books.

Cutler, S., 1973. Voluntary association participation and life satisfaction. *Journal of Gerontology*, 28:96-100.

Cutler, S., 1975. Transportation and changes in life satisfaction. *Gerontologist*, 15:155-159.

Cutler, S., 1976a. Age differences in voluntary association memberships. *Social Forces,* 55:43-58.

Cutler, S., 1976b. Membership in different types of voluntary associations and psychological well-being. *Gerontologist.* 16:335-339.

Cutler, S., 1977. Aging and voluntary association participation. *Journal of Gerontology,* 32:470-479.

Dohrenwend, B. S., & Dohrenwend, B. P. (Eds.), 1974. *Stressful life events.* New York: Wiley.

Edwards, J., & Klemmack, D., 1973. Correlates of life satisfaction. *Journal of Gerontology.* 28:497-502.

Erskine, H. 1965. The polls. *Public Opinion Quarterly,* 29:679.

Finkle, A., Moyers, T., Tobenkin, M., et al., 1969. Sexual potency in aging males. *Journal of American Medical Association,* 170:113-115.

Fox, J., 1979. Challenging the canons of continuity. Paper presented at annual meeting of Gerontological Society, Washington, D.C.

Freeman, J., 1961. Sexual capacities in the aging male. *Geriatrics,* 16:37-43.

Fried, E., Rivlin, A., Schultze, C., & Teeters, N., 1973. *Setting national priorities.* Washington, D.C.: Brookings Institute.

Fukuyama, Y., 1961. The major dimensions of church membership. *Review of Religious Research,* 2:154-161.

George, L., 1978. Predictors of activity and morale patterns in late life. *Journal of Gerontology,* 33:840-847.

George, L., & Weiler, S. (in press). Sexuality in middle and late life. *Archives of General Psychiatry.*

Glenn, N., & Grimes, M., 1968. Aging, voting, and political interest. *American Sociological Review,* 33:563-575.

Gordon, C., & Gaitz, C., 1976. Leisure and lives. In R. Binstock and E. Shanas (Eds.), *Handbook of aging and the social sciences.* New York: Van Nostrand Reinhold Co.

Gurin, G., Veroff, J., & Field, S., 1960. *Americans view their mental health.* New York: Basic Books.

Harris, L., 1975. *The myth and reality of aging in America.* Washington, D.C.: National Council on the Aging.

Havighurst, R., 1957. The social competence of middle-aged people. *Genetic Psychological Monographs,*56:297-375.

Havighurst, R., 1973. Social roles, work, leisure, and education. In C. Eisdorfer and M. Lawton (Eds.), *The psychology of adult development and aging.* Washington, D.C.: American Psychological Association.

Havighurst, R., Neugarten, B., Munnichs, J., & Thomas, H. (Eds.), 1969. *Adjustment to retirement.* Netherlands: Van Gorkum.

Havighurst, R., 1963. Successful aging. In R. Williams, C. Tibbitts, and W. Donahue (Eds.), *Processes of aging.* New York: Atherton Press.

Henretta, J., & Campbell, R., 1976. Status attainment and status maintenance. *American Sociological Review* 41:981-992.

Henretta, J., & Campbell, R., 1978. Net work as an aspect of status. *American Journal of Sociology,* 41:981-92.

Holmes, T., & Rahe, R., 1967. The social readjustment scale. *Journal of Psychosomatic Research,* 11:213-218.

House, J., 1974. Occupational stress and coronary heart disease. *Journal of Health and Social Behavior,* 15:12-27.

Hudson, R., & Binstock, R., 1976. Political systems and aging. In R. Binstock and E. Shanas (Eds.), *Handbook of aging and the social sciences.* New York: Van Nostrand Reinhold Co.

Hunter, W., & Maurice, H., 1953. *Older people tell their story.* Ann Arbor: University of Michigan, Division of Gerontology.

Jacobson, D., 1972. Willingness to retire in relation to job strain and type of work. *Industrial Gerontology,* 13:65-74.

Johnson, M., 1975. Voluntary affifiation: Changing age patterns? *American Sociological Association 1975 Annual Proceedings*, 209-210.

Kelly, E., 1955. Consistency of the adult personality. *American Psychologist*, 10:659-81.

Kinsey, A., Pomeroy, W., & Martin, C., 1948. *Sexual behavior in the human male*. Philadelphia: Saunders.

Kinsey, A., Pomeroy, W., Martin, C., & Gibhard, P., 1953. *Sexual behavior in the human female*. Philadelphia: Saunders.

Kivett, V., 1976. *The aged in North Carolina*. N.C. Agricultural Experiment Station, Tech. Bul. N237.

Kutner, B., 1956. *Five hundred over sixty*. New York: Russell Sage Foundation.

Larson, R., 1975. Is satisfaction with life the same in different subcultures: Unpublished manuscript.

Larson, R., 1978. Thirty years of research on the subjective well-being of older Americans. *Journal of Gerontology*, 33:109-129.

Lawton, M., 1972. The dimensions of morale. In D. Kent, R. Kastenbaum, and S. Sherwood (Eds.), *Research planning and action for the elderly*. New York: Behavioral Publications.

Lawton, M., & Cohen, J., 1974. Housing impact on older people. *Journal of Gerontology*, 29:194-204.

Lebo, D., 1953. Some factors said to make for happiness in old age. *Journal of Clinical Psychology*, 9:384-390.

Lee, G., 1979. Children and the elderly. *Research on Aging*, 1:335-359.

Lemon, B., Benston, V., & Peterson, J., 1972. An exploration of the activity theory of aging. *Journal of Gerontology*, 27:511-523.

Lopata, H., 1973. *Widowhood in an American city*. Cambridge, Mass.: Schenkmen.

Lowenthal, M., & Berkman, P., 1967. *Aging and mental disorder in San Francisco*. San Francisco: Jossey-Bass.

Lowenthal, M., & Havens, C., 1968. Interaction and adaptation. *American Sociological Review*, 33:20-30.

Lowenthal, M., Thurner, M., & Chiriboga, D., 1975. *Four stages of life*. San Francisco: Jossey-Bass.

Lowry, J., 1979. Evidence on the impact of mandatory retirement for individual's activity level, life satisfaction, and adjustment rating. Paper presented to annual meeting of the American Sociological Association, Boston.

Maddox, G., 1962. A longitudinal, multidisciplinary study of human aging. *Proceedings of The American Statistical Association*, 1962:280-285.

Maddox, G., 1970. Persistence of life style among the elderly. In E. Palmore (Ed.), *Normal aging*. Durham, N.C.: Duke University Press.

Maddox, G., & Douglas, E., 1974. Aging and individual differences. *Journal of Gerontology*, 29:555-563.

Maddox, G., & Wiley, J., 1976. Scope, concepts, and methods in the study of aging. In R. Binstock and E. Shanas (Eds.), *Handbook of aging and the social sciences*. New York: Van Nostrand Reinhold.

Martin, W., 1973. Activity and disengagement. *Gerontologist*, 13:224-227.

Masters, W., & Johnson, V., 1966. *Human sexual response*. Boston: Little Brown.

Masters, W., & Johnson, V., 1970. *Human sexual inadequacy*. Boston: Little Brown.

Miller, H., 1965. Lifetime income and economic growth. *American Economic Review*, 55:834-844.

Myers, R., 1965. Factors in interpreting mortality after retirement. *Journal of American Statistical Association*, 49:499-509.

Nadelson, T., 1969. A survey of the literature on the adjustment of the aged to retirement. *Journal of Geriatric Psychiatry*, 3:3-20.

Neugarten, B., 1964. *Personality in middle and later life*. New York: Atherton Press.

Neugarten, B., Havighurst, R., & Tobin, S., 1961. The measurement of life satisfaction. *Journal of Gerontology*, 16:134-143.

Newman, G., & Nichols, C., 1960. Sexual activities and attitudes in older persons *Journal of American Medical Association*, 173:33-35.

Nie, N., Verba, S., & Kim, J., 1974. Political participation and the life cycle. *Comparative politics*, 6:319-340.

Owens, W., 1966. Age and mental abilities. *Journal of Educational Psychology*, 57:311-325.

Palmore, E., 1952. Published reactions to the Kinsey Report. *Social Forces*, 31:165-172.

Palmore, E., 1967. Employment and retirement. In L. Epstein (Ed.), *The aged population of the United States*, Washington: U.S. Government Printing Office.

Palmore, E., (Ed.), 1970. *Normal aging*. Durham, N.C.: Duke University Press.

Palmore, E., 1971a. The relative importance of social factors in predicting longevity. In E. Palmore and F. Jeffers (Eds.), *Prediction of life span*. Lexington, Mass.: Heath Lexington Books.

Palmore, E., 1971b. Why do people retire? *Aging and Human Development*, 2:269-283.

Palmore E., 1973. Social factors in mental illness of the aged. In E. Busse and E. Pfeiffer (Eds.), *Mental illness in later life*. Washington American Psychiatric Association.

Palmore, E. (Ed.), 1974. *Normal aging II*. Durham, N.C.: Duke University Press.

Palmore, E., 1976a. The future status of the aged. *Gerontologist*, 16:297-302.

Palmore, E., 1976b. Total chance of institutionalization among the aged. *Gerontologist*, 16:504-507.

Palmore, E., 1977. Facts on aging: a short quiz. *Gerontologist*, 17:315-320.

Palmore, E., 1978a. When can age, period, and cohort be separated? *Social Forces*, 57:282-295.

Palmore, E., 1978b. Are the aged a minority group? *Journal of the American Geriatric Society*, 26:214-217.

Palmore, E., 1979a. Social factors in aging. In E. Busse and D. Blazer (Eds.), *Handbook of geriatric psychiatry*. New York: Van Nostrand Reinhold.

Palmore, E., 1979b. Predictors of successful aging. *Gerontologist*, 19:427-431.

Palmore, E., Cleveland, W., Nowlin, J., Ramm, D., & Siegler, I., 1979. Stress and adaptation in later life. *Journal of Gerontology*, 31:841-845.

Palmore, E., & Jeffers, F. (Eds.), 1971. *Prediction of life span*. Lexington, Mass.: D.C. Heath.

Palmore E., & Kivett, V., 1977. Change in life satisfaction. *Journal of Gerontology*. 32:311-316.

Palmore, E., & Luikart, C., 1974. Health and social factors related to life satisfaction. In E. Palmore (Ed.) *Normal aging II*. Durham, N.C.: Duke University Press.

Palmore, E., & Stone, V., 1973. Predictors of longevity. *Gerontologist*, 13:88-90.

Pfeiffer, E., & Davis, G., 1972. Determinants of sexual behavior in middle and old age. *Journal of American Geriatrics Society*, 20:4:151-158.

Pfeiffer, E., Verwoerdt, A., & Davis, G., 1972. Sexual behavior in middle life. *American Journal of Psychiatry*, 128:82-87.

Pfeiffer, E., Verwoerdt, A., & Wang, H., 1968. *Archives of General Psychiatry*, 19:756-758.

Phillips, B., 1957. A role theory approach to adjustment in old age. *American Sociological Review*, 22:212-217.

Reichard, S., Livson, F., & Peterson, P., 1962. *Aging and personality*. New York: John Wiley.

Reno, V., 1971. Why men stop working at or before age 65. *Social Security Bulletin*, 34:3-17.

Riegel, K., 1971. The prediction of death and longevity in longitudinal research. In E. Palmore and F. Jeffers (Eds.), *Prediction of life span*. Lexington, Mass.: Heath Lexington.

Riegel, K., Riegel, R., & Meyer, G., 1967. Socio-psychological factors of aging. *Human Development*. 10:27-56.

Riley, M., & Foner, A., 1968. *Aging and society, vol. 1: An inventory of research findings*. New York: Russell Sage Foundation.

Riley, M., Johnson, M., & Foner, A., 1972. *Aging and society, vol. 3*. New York: Russell Sage Foundation.

Rose, A., & Peterson, W., 1965. *Older people and their social world.* Philadelphia, Pa.: F. A. Davis.

Rosenberg, G., 1970. *The worker grows old.* San Francisco: Jossey-Bass.

Rosow, I., 1967. *Social integration of the aged.* New York: Free Press.

Rozelle, R., & Campbell, D., 1969. More plausible rival hypotheses in the cross-lagged panel technique. *Psychological Bulletin.* 71:74-84.

Schooler, K., 1969. The relationship between social interaction and morale of the elderly as a function of environmental characteristics. *Gerontologist,* 9:25-29.

Schultz, J., 1976. Income distribution and the aging. In R. Binstock and E. Shanas, (Eds.), *Handbook of aging and the social sciences.* New York: Van Nostrand Reinhold.

Scotch, N., & Richardson, A., 1966. Characteristics of the self-sufficient among the very aged. *Proceedings, 7th International Congress of Gerontology,* Vienna, 8:489-493.

Shanas, E., 1979. The family as a social support system in old age. *Gerontologist,* 19:169-174.

Shanas, E., Townsend, P., Wedderbum, D., Friis, H., Milhot, P., & Stehovwer, J. 1968. *Older people in three industrial societies,* New York: Atherton Press.

Sheldon, H., 1958. *The older population of the U.S.* New York: Wiley.

Sheppard, H., 1972. *Where have all the robots gone?* New York: The Free Press.

Sheppard, H., 1976. Work and retirement. In R. Binstock and E. Shanas (Eds.), *Handbook of aging and the social sciences,* New York: Van Nostrand Reinhold.

Simpson, I., & McKinney, J. (Eds.), 1966. *Social aspects of aging.* Durham, N.C.: Duke University Press.

Smith, K., & Lipman, A., 1972. Constraint and life satisfaction. *Journal of Gerontology,* 27:77-82.

Spreitzer, E., & Snyder, E., 1974. Correlates of life satisfaction among the aged. *Journal of Gerontology,* 29:454-458.

Streib, G., & Schneider, C., 1971. *Retirement in American society.* Ithaca, N.Y.: Cornell University Press.

Surrey, S., 1973. *Pathways to tax reform.* Cambridge, Mass.: Harvard University Press.

Tallmer, M., & Kutner, B., 1970. Disengagement and morale. *Gerontologist,* 10:4, Part 1, 317-320.

Tobin, S., & Neugarten, B., 1961. Life satisfaction and social interaction in the aging. *Journal of Gerontology.* 16:344-346.

Verba, S., & Nie, N., 1972. *Participation in America.* New York: Harper & Row.

Verwoerdt, A., Pfeiffer, E., & Wang, H., 1969. Sexual behavior in senescence, II. *Geriatrics,* 20:137-154.

Videbeck, C., & Knox, A., 1965. Alternative participatory responses to aging. In Rose, A., and Peterson, W. (Eds.), *Older people and their social world.* Philadelphia: F. A. Davis.

Ward, R., 1979. The meaning of voluntary association participation to older people. *Journal of Gerontology,* 34:438-445.

Weber, M., 1947. *The theory of social and economic organization.* Glencoe, Ill.: The Free Press.

Wechsler, D., 1955. *Manual for the Wechsler Adult Intelligence Scale.* New York: Psychological Corporation.

Youmans, E., 1962. *Leisure time activities of older persons in selected rural and urban areas of Kentucky.* Progress Report 115, Kentucky Agricultural Experiment Station, Lexington, Ky.

Index

Achievement values, 58, 77, 95, 117
Activity, 9, 26, 42-43, 58, 60, 62, 101, 103, 105-106, 117, 118, 121, 125, 126; primary group, 56, 57, 58, 66, 102, 123; secondary group, 56, 57, 62, 66, 103, 124. *See also* Political, Religious, Sexual, Social, and Solitary activity.
Activity theory, 4, 60-61, 64, 109
Affect balance, 30, 44, 63, 95, 98, 102, 103, 106, 117
Age stratification, 4-5, 110. *See also* Cohorts
Aging, successful, 95, 102-103, 106
Anderson, B., 75, 79, 95, 96
Andrews, F., 96
Anomie, 95, 98, 99, 102, 103, 105, 106, 107, 117-118
Atchley, R., 4, 17, 41, 48, 74, 79
Aucoin, J., 61

Babchuck, N., 48
Barfield, R., 37
Bartko, J., 61
Bell, R., 48, 79
Bengtson, V., 60
Berardo, F., 79
Berkman, P., 25, 41, 55, 61
Binstock, R., 16, 48
Blau, Z., 79
Booth, A., 48
Botwinick, J., 25
Bradburn, N., 95, 117
Bromley, D., 49
Bull, C., 61
Burgess, E., 48, 60, 120, 121, 126
Butler, R., 61

Cameron, P., 7, 49
Campbell, A., 95, 96
Campbell, R., 17, 22, 23
Cantril, H., 95
Caplovitz, D., 95, 117
Carp, F., 100
Cavan, R., 48, 120, 121, 126
Children: and life satisfaction, 44-45; and SES, 23, 24, 26, 31; and social activity, 57, 58; and social networks, 70, 72, 74, 75, 76, 78, 79, 80, 81, 82, 109; variables relating to, defined, 118, 119
Chiriboga, D., 74, 75, 95, 96
Clark, M., 75, 79, 95, 96
Cleveland, W., 13, 42, 79
Cognitive function: and health, 112; and life satisfaction, 101, 103; and SES, 25, 29, 30,

31; and social activity, 56, 58; variables relating to, defined, 122, 123, 126
Cohen, J., 100
Cohorts 4, 5, 11, 15, 47
Confidant, 61, 69-70, 78, 80, 103, 104, 118
Continuity theory, 4, 49, 53-54, 109
Converse, P., 95, 96
Cottrell, F., 41
Cronbrack, L., 13
Cumming, E., 3, 4, 47, 55, 60, 61
Cutler, S., 26, 48, 55, 61, 100

Davis, G., 84, 91
Death, 4, 6, 7, 40, 49
Disability, 31, 37, 38, 110, 111
Discrimination, 6, 16, 35, 39, 110, 111, 115
Disengagement theory, 3-4, 43, 47, 48, 52, 60-61, 108-109
Dohrenwend, B. P., 6
Dohrenwend, B. S., 6
Douglas, E., 6, 49

Education, 115; and adaptation, 30; and income, 22, 23, 24, 31; and mental health, 25; and retirement, 37; and social activity, 55, 56, 58; and social networks, 75, 77, 78; as cohort effect, 15, 31, 110, 113; as predictor, 101, 102, 103, 105; as SES measure, 27, 29; of sample members, 10, 11, 17
Edwards, J., 26, 96
Employment, 16, 70, 116; and income, 23; and life satisfaction, 101, 107; and longevity, 64, 65; and social activity, 56, 57; and social networks, 75, 77; and social problems, 26; as variable, defined, 119; discrimination in, 35; *vs.* retirement, 32, 39. *See also* Occupation; Retirement
"Empty nest" syndrome, 79, 82, 109, 112, 114
Erskine, H., 48

Field, S., 79, 95
Financial status, 16-17, 19-20, 26, 28, 100, 101, 102, 103, 107, 116, 118, 119. *See also* Income; Poverty
Finkle, A., 83
Foner, A., 4, 24, 25, 48, 75
Fox, J., 54
Free time, 43, 119
Freeman, J., 83
Fried, E., 16
Friends, 26, 29, 31, 41, 42, 47-48, 52, 61, 65, 69, 70, 72, 73, 75, 76, 78, 79-80, 109, 111, 118, 119

Friis, H., 74, 76, 79
Furby, L., 13
Fukuyama, Y., 48

Gaitz, C., 47, 48, 55
George L., 44, 48
Gianturco, D., 79
Gibhard, P., 83, 89
Glenn, N., 48
Goldhamer, H., 48, 120, 121, 126
Gordon, C., 47, 48, 55
Grimes, M., 48
Gurin, G., 79, 95, 96

Happiness. *See* Life satisfaction
Harris, L., 15, 16, 24, 26, 37, 48, 55, 69, 74, 96
Havens, C., 61, 80
Havighurst, R., 4, 26, 48, 49, 55, 60, 120, 121, 126
Health, mental: and life satisfaction, 104; and retirement, 41; and SES, 25, 29, 30, 31; and sexual behavior, 93; and social activity, 59; and social networks, 81; and stress theory, 111, 112
Health, physical: and life satisfaction, 99-100, 101, 102, 103, 105-106, 107; and poverty, 25; and prejudice, 115; and religious activity, 57; and retirement, 34, 36, 38, 40-41, 42, 113; and SES, 24, 26, 30, 31; and sexual behavior, 92, 94; and social activity, 54, 56, 59, 61, 62-63, 64, 65, 66, 109; and social networks, 75, 76, 77, 80, 81, 82, 109; of sample, 9, 10, 109
Henretta, J., 17, 22, 23
Henry, W., 3, 4, 47, 55, 60, 61
Heyman, D., 79
Holmes, T., 79
Homogeneity *vs.* heterogeneity, 6, 48-49, 53, 65, 70, 89, 94, 99, 107, 112-113, 114
Homosexuality, 89, 90
Horr, D., 48
House, J., 6
Housing, 25, 26, 100
Hudson, R., 48
Hunter, W., 75

Income: and affect balance, 27; and health, 27; and homogeneity, 112, 113; and longitudinal studies, 113; and life satisfaction, 26, 27, 95, 101, 103; and minority group theory, 111, 115; and retirement, 37, 40, 43; and SES, 15, 16, 17-19, 20, 22-23, 27, 29, 30; and social activity, 26, 27, 29, 55, 58, 59; and social networks, 29, 77, 78; as aging effect, 16, 17, 31, 110, 113; as cohort effect, 16, 17, 31, 110, 113; as variable, defined, 120. *See also* Financial status
Institutionalization, 7, 79, 81, 111
Intelligence. *See* Cognitive function
Internal control, 58, 59, 103, 105, 121

Jacobson, D., 38
Jeffers, F., 74
Johnson, M., 4, 48
Johnson, V., 83, 89, 90

Kaiser, M., 48
Kelley, E., 49
Kim, J., 48
Kinsey, A., 83, 89, 90
Kivett, V., 96
Klemmack, D., 26, 96
Knox, A., 48, 49
Kutner, B., 26, 47, 55, 60, 61, 74, 79, 95, 96

Larson, R., 95, 96, 99
Lawton, M., 96, 100
Lebo, D., 60
Lee, G., 79
Lemon, B., 60
Life events stress theory, 4, 6, 111-112
Life satisfaction, 95-107; and affect balance, 98, 99, 101, 102; and aging effects, 95, 96, 106, 107, 110; and anomie, 98, 102, 105, 107; and happiness, 97-98, 101, 105, 106; and health, 104, 106; and health self-rating, 100, 101, 105; and homogeneity, 99, 107, 113; and income, 100, 101, 107; and retirement, 41, 43, 44-45, 109, 111; and SES, 26, 29, 30, 95, 100, 107; and sex differences, 100; and sexual behavior, 91, 92, 93, 94, 95, 100, 107, 114; and social activity, 60-61, 62-63, 65, 66, 100, 103, 104, 105, 106, 109; and social networks, 80, 81, 105, 109; and widowhood, 79, 109; as variable, defined; 121, previous research on, 95-96, 99-100
Lipman, A., 100
Living arrangements, 41, 116; and cohort effects, 114; and social activity, 54, 55, 56, 58, 65, 66; and social networks, 67-69, 70, 71, 73, 74, 75-76, 78, 80-81; *household*, as variable, defined, 120
Livson, F., 60
Loneliness, 26, 42, 69, 117
Longevity: and Duke studies' methodology, 8, 11, 13; and retirement, 40-41; and SES, 25, 31; and sexual behavior, 93; and social activity, 61, 62, 66
Longitudinal methodology, 5, 7-14, 42-43, 44, 55-56, 108, 113-114
Lopata, H., 79
Lowenthal, M., 25, 41, 54, 55, 61, 74, 75, 80, 95, 96
Lowry, J., 44
Luikart, C., 42n, 44

McKinney, J., 37, 41, 42
Maddox, G., 6, 9, 49, 61
Marital status: aging and cohort effects of, 114; and health, 80, 110; and income, 22-23, 31;

and life satisfaction, 102, 107; and retirement, 37; and SES, 74; and sexual behavior, 84, 90, 91, 93, 94; and social activity, 54, 55, 65; and social networks, 73-74; of sample members, 10, 11, 70, 71; trends in, 67-69, 70, 71. *See* Widowhood
Martin, C., 83, 89
Martin, W., 100
Masters, W., 83, 89, 90
Masturbation, 87, 89
Maurice, H., 75
Medical care, 24-25, 31, 115-116
Medication, 42, 122
Meyer, G., 49
Middle-age, 6, 9, 45, 65, 81, 111, 114
Milhot, P., 74, 76, 79
Miller, H., 16
Minority group theory, 5-6, 110-111
Morale. *See* Life satisfaction
Morgan, J., 37
Moyers, T., 83
Myers, R., 40

Nadelson, T., 41
Neugarten, B., 4, 6, 26, 96
Newman, G., 84
Nichols, G., 84
Nie, N., 48
Nowlin, J., 13, 42, 79

Occupation: and income, 23, 24, 31; and retirement, 37-38; and SES, 15-16, 22, 23, 27, 28, 29; and social activity, 56, 58; and social networks, 75, 76, 77; as cohort effect, 15-16, 31, 110, 113; as variable, defined, 122; of sample members, 11, 17, 18
Old age identification, 34, 38, 58, 78, 123

Palmore, E., 3, 5, 6, 9, 10, 11, 15, 16, 25, 32, 33, 34, 37, 42, 44, 48, 74, 79, 83, 96, 102
Patterson, R., 61
Peters, G., 48
Peterson, J., 60
Peterson, P., 60
Peterson, W., 72
Pfeiffer, E., 84, 90, 91
Phillips, B., 60
Political activity, 48, 65
Pomeroy, W., 83, 89
Poverty, 4, 16, 17, 24, 25, 40, 46, 110-111, 115
Psychosomatic symptoms, 26, 28, 30, 42, 124

Racial group differences, 4, 55, 56, 57, 74, 76, 81, 100, 107, 124
Rahe, R., 79
Ramm, D., 13, 42, 79
Reichard, S., 60
Relatives: and life satisfaction, 61; and SES, 26, 29, 31; and social activity, 47-48, 52, 57, 58, 65, 111; and social networks, 69, 70, 73, 74,

75, 76, 78, 81; variables relating to, defined, 119, 124
Religious activity: and life satisfaction, 101; and retirement, 42, 46; and SES, 26, 29, 31, 57, 66; and sexual behavior, 89; and social activity, 56, 58-59; as aging effect, 52-53, 54, 65, 108; as cohort effect, 48; variables relating to, defined, 118, 124
Reno, V., 37
Retirement, 32-46, 108; and health, 38, 39, 40, 41, 42, 109, 111, 113; and homogeneity, 112; and income, 37, 40-41, 113; and life satisfaction, 41, 44, 45, 109, 111, 113; and marital status, 37; and occupation, 37, 38; and SES, 16, 17, 20, 31; and social activity, 41, 42, 46, 51, 52; and social networks, 70, 80; as cohort effect, 32, 33; consequences of, 39-45; defined, 32; determinants of, 34-39; mandatory, 33, 37, 38, 44, 45, 46, 61, 109, 111, 113, 115; rate of, 32, 33, 34, 36, 37
Richardson, A., 54, 55
Riegel, K., 49
Riegel, R., 49
Riley, M., 4, 24, 25, 48, 75
Rivlin, A., 16
Rodgers, W., 95, 96
Role theory, 37
Rose, A., 72
Rosenberg, G., 74, 79, 80
Rosow, I., 60, 74, 75

Schneider, C., 16, 17, 20, 37, 40, 41
Schooler, K., 100
Schultz, J., 16, 23
Schultze, C., 16
Scotch, N., 54, 55
Sex differences: and homogeneity, 6-7, 49, 112: and life satisfaction, 100-101, 107; and retirement, 32-34, 37-37, 38-39, 110; and social activity, 51, 52, 55, 57, 58, 66; and social networks, 67-68, 78, 79
Sexual activity, 83-94, 100; and affect balance, 102, 104; and anomie, 103; and health, 93, 109, 114; and homogeneity, 49, 112-113; and life satisfaction, 93, 94, 101, 102, 107, 114; and religious activity, 89; and SES, 89, 90; and sex differences, 89, 90, 91, 92, 93, 94; as aging effect, 83-89, 109, 111; as cohort effect, 90; antecedents of, 89-92; predictors of, 91, 114; previous research on, 83-84, 89; variables relating to, defined, 120, 123, 125
Shanas, E., 16, 74, 76, 79
Sheldon, H., 73
Sheppard, H., 38
Siegler, I., 13, 42, 79
Simpson, I., 37, 41, 42
Smith, K., 100
Smoking, 64, 102
Snyder, E., 26, 96
Social activity, 4, 47-66; and aging effects, 49,

51, 52, 53, 54, 56, 65, 108, 109, 110, 111; and homogeneity, 48, 53, 65, 112; and race, 56, 67 and religious activity, 48; and retirement, 41-42, 46; and SES, 25-26, 29, 30-31, 55, 66; and sex differences, 50, 56, 58; predictors of, 58, 65; previous research on, 47-49, 54-55, 59-61; consequences of, 59-65, 66, 100, 102, 103, 104, 109; variables relating to, defined, 122, 123, 125, 126

Social networks, 59, 67-82, 108, 109, 112, 113, 126

Socioeconomic status, 4, 5, 15-31; and affect balance, 29; and cognitive function, 25, 29, 31; and education, 15, 17, 24, 29, 31; and happiness, 29; and health, 24, 25, 29, 30, 31, 41, 113; and income, 16, 17, 18, 19, 22, 24, 31; and life satisfaction, 26, 30, 31, 100, 101-102, 107, 113; and longevity, 25; and religious activity, 29, 31, 57; and retirement, 41; and sexual behavior, 89, 91, 92, 94; and social activity, 25, 29, 30, 31, 55, 57, 58-59, 61, 66; and social networks, 29, 31, 74, 76, 77, 78, 81; as aging effect, 110; as cohort effect, 110, 113; class identification, as variable, defined, 118; of sample members, 9, 17, 18, 19; previous research on, 15-17, 22-23, 24-26; subjective perception of, 20-21

Solitary activity, 42, 43, 51, 55, 103, 125-126

Spreitzer, E., 26, 96

Status feelings, 15, 20-22, 31, 58, 95, 103, 113, 124

Stehovwer, J., 74, 76, 79

Stone, V., 25

Streib, G., 16, 17, 20, 37, 40, 41

Stress theory. *See* Life events stress theory

Suicide, 79

Surrey, S., 16

Tallmer, M., 55, 61

Teeters, N., 16

Thurner, M., 74, 75, 95, 96

Tobenkin, M., 83

Tobin, S., 26

Townsend, P., 74, 76, 79

Useful, feeling, 95, 119

Verba, S., 48

Veroff, J., 79, 95

Verwoerdt, A., 84, 90, 91

Videbeck, C., 48, 49

Wang, H., 84, 90, 91

Ward, R., 61

Weber, M., 15

Wechsler, D., 123

Wedderbum, D., 74, 76, 79

Weiler, S., 84

Widowhood, 42, 61, 67-68, 70, 73-74, 75, 78, 79, 80, 81, 84, 93, 109, 111-112, 114

Withey, S., 96

Work satisfaction, 64, 95, 103, 126

Youmans, E., 47

Younger persons, 70, 72-73, 81, 114, 115, 119. *See also* Children

About the Author

Erdman Palmore is Professor of Medical Sociology, Duke University. He is editor of *Normal Aging I* and *Normal Aging II* (Reports from the Duke Longitudinal Studies) and author of *The Honorable Elders: A Cross-Cultural Analysis of Aging in Japan,* all published by Duke University Press. Dr. Palmore has edited and contributed to *International Handbook on Aging* and *Prediction of Life Span* and has published widely in other books and scholarly journals on aspects of aging.

Books in Gerontology from Duke University Press

Normal Aging I

Reports from the Duke Longitudinal Studies, 1955-1969

Erdman Palmore, *editor*

Normal Aging II

Reports from the Duke Longitudinal Studies, 1970-1973

Erdman Palmore, *editor*

The Honorable Elders

A Cross-Cultural Analysis of Aging in Japan

Erdman Palmore

Retirement Policy in an Aging Society

Robert L. Clark, *editor*

Family, Bureaucracy, and the Elderly

Ethel Shanas and Marvin B. Sussman, *editors*

Social Aspects of Aging

Ida Harper Simpson and John C. McKinney, *editors*

Lifetime Allocation of Work and Income

Essays in the Economics of Aging

Juanita M. Kreps

Employment, Income, and Retirement Problems of the Aged

Juanita M. Kreps, *editor*